Faith over Fear

OVERCOMING FEAR BY FAITH

Charity A. Lane

WESTBOW
PRESS®
A DIVISION OF THOMAS NELSON
& ZONDERVAN

This book is a work of non-fiction. Unless otherwise noted, the author and the publisher make no explicit guarantees as to the accuracy of the information contained in this book and in some cases, names of people and places have been altered to protect their privacy.

HCSB:
Scripture quotations marked HCSB are taken from the Holman Christian Standard Bible®, Copyright © 1999, 2000, 2002, 2003, 2009 by Holman Bible Publishers. Used by permission. Holman Christian Standard Bible®, Holman CSB®, and HCSB® are federally registered trademarks of Holman Bible Publishers.
NLT:
Scripture quotations marked (NLT) are taken from the Holy Bible, New Living Translation, copyright © 1996, 2004, 2007 by Tyndale House Foundation. Used by permission of Tyndale House Publishers, Inc., Carol Stream, Illinois 60188. All rights reserved.
KJV:
Scripture taken from the King James Version of the Bible.
NKJV:
Scripture taken from the New King James Version®. Copyright © 1982 by Thomas Nelson. Used by permission. All rights reserved.

WestBow Press books may be ordered through booksellers or by contacting:

WestBow Press
A Division of Thomas Nelson & Zondervan
1663 Liberty Drive
Bloomington, IN 47403
www.westbowpress.com
1 (866) 928-1240

ISBN: 978-1-9736-2746-3 (sc)
ISBN: 978-1-9736-2745-6 (hc)
ISBN: 978-1-9736-2747-0 (e)

Library of Congress Control Number: 2018905429

Print information available on the last page.

WestBow Press rev. date: 06/25/2018

Contents

Faith and Fear

Stand Firm—Foundations of Faith

Strong in Faith

Faith
and
Fear

Introduction

Christian author James Hastings wrote, "Fear is the needle that pierces us that it may carry a thread to bind us to heaven."

The first time I read those words, I knew exactly what Hastings meant because I have felt the disabling prick of the needle of fear. At one point in my life, I thought the needle of fear might just be the death of me, but in that darkest moment, I stumbled upon the thread I believe Hastings spoke of, the simple promise that my faith in my heavenly Father could conquer my fear.

Over time, the thread of faith that was born out of my darkest moments with fear became my own personal victory over fear by binding me to my heavenly Father and to heaven in ways that I never imagined were possible.

I want to share with you what I have learned so far through my own lifelong struggle with fear. If you'll join me on this journey, we'll take a thorough look at the needle of fear so we can clearly see the holes that it pierces in our hearts, our minds, and our souls. Then we'll bind ourselves to heaven by weaving a triple-braided thread of faith through our hearts with trust, our minds with peace, and our souls with hope.

Chapter 1

Fortune and Faith

As a young child, I often woke up from a dead sleep in the late hours of the night, terrified beyond reason. But it was not of anything in particular. It was everything. Alone, I would lie there shaking in my bed, afraid to move and almost too scared to breathe. It seemed as though I could almost feel the darkness swirling around me, as if the inky blackness of the night air were alive and closing in on me.

In the midst of that nightmarish terror, I knew that my only hope of peace lay at the other end of my family's small home. He was sound asleep in his own bed. I knew that, if I could gain just enough courage to jump out of my bed and run down the hallway, through the living room, and into my parents' bedroom, my father would rescue me. He would wrap me in his arms, pull me close, and whisper, "Don't be afraid." Then, as if by magic, my fears would fade.

So grabbing my blanket to use as a shield against all the terrifying creatures of the night, I would gather what little courage I could muster and run as fast as I could through the ever-thickening darkness to my father. And when I got to him, he would gently pull me close and whisper in my ear, "Don't be afraid." Then all my fears would fade away as if they had never existed ... for a time at least.

As I grew out of childhood, I eventually learned to sleep in my own bed at night, but the paralyzing fear that surfaced in the earliest years of my life never quite left me in peace. In fact, fear became a more powerful force in my life than I ever realized it could be.

The fear that had awakened me in the darkness of the night began to follow me through the light of day. Worry became a constant companion, anxiety was an unwanted friend who stuck closer than a brother, and panic was the crazy uncle who occasionally dropped in on my life unannounced, leaving a trail of chaos and despair in his wake.

Fear overwhelmed my life, and I feared that one day it would completely engulf me in its power until, surprisingly enough, I found the peace that I so desperately needed in much the same place that I had found it as a young child, my Father's embrace and whispered words of peace.

A Hope-Filled Fortune

I was pregnant for the second time, and though doctors had assured me that a second pregnancy wouldn't be nearly as difficult as my first had been, my body was proving them wrong. I felt deathly ill. I was scared to death and literally terrified of death.

One night, in spite of my physical and spiritual discomfort, my pregnancy cravings called for Chinese food. The food didn't satisfy my heart's desire for comfort and peace, but something else I found that night did.

Packed up in the brown paper bag, alongside my General Tso's chicken, was a fortune cookie. This was no ordinary fortune cookie. When I gently cracked it open and read the words inside, I knew with more certainly than I had ever known before in my life that I had heard the voice of God. The tiny slip of paper nestled in that fortune cookie read, "May my faith always exceed my fears. The price is too great to go through life afraid."

My very pregnant and extremely emotional state got the best of me as tears streamed down my face and into my plate of fried rice and spicy chicken. I was undeniably familiar with the too great price of going through life afraid. I had been living that truth for most of my life. The first part of the statement, however, really captured my attention. I began to wonder why my faith wasn't exceeding my fears.

Why was the faith in God that I had proclaimed since early childhood failing me in the area I needed it the most and leaving me to pay the too great price of struggling through life in emotional and spiritual turmoil while being afraid?

At that time in my life, I probably read proverbs from fortune cookies more often than I read my Bible, hence the need for God to speak to me in such as absurd manner. And I immediately knew that was at least part of the problem behind my failing faith.

Conviction embraced me, and I began to wonder if the answers I knew I so desperately needed in my life could be found in the Word of God that had collected dust in the top drawer of my nightstand. In perhaps the darkest season of my life, at the urging of an extraordinary fortune cookie, I cracked open my Bible with an anticipation born of a hope that I had nearly forgotten I possessed.

I don't remember exactly what I found the first time I searched for insight into my seemingly powerless faith in scripture, but I do remember the comfort that came as I pored over God's words that night. And I remember the unexplainable peace that enveloped me like a warm embrace from my heavenly Father.

That elusive peace and peculiar comfort kept me running back to the pages of scripture in the very midst of my spiritual turmoil. There, in quiet moments with God and His Word, I began to feel my heavenly Father wrap His arms around me, pull me close, and whisper the very same sentiment my earthly father had whispered so many years earlier when I ran to him in the midst of my fears. "Fear not."

"Fear not" is how God says, "Don't be afraid" in the King James Version of scripture. And He says it a lot. In fact, that simple phrase of assurance appears more than any other in scripture. It is spoken by angels, prophets, Jesus during his ministry on this Earth, and even the very voice of God ringing out from the heavens.

I believe that the many scripture appearances of the phrase "Fear not" is our heavenly Father's way of whispering to each of His children as many times as we might need to hear it in the darkness of this world, "Don't be afraid." But in His infinite wisdom, God doesn't stop there. He reveals in scripture that it is entirely possible for us to completely overcome fear in this life.

Faith versus Fear

The beloved apostle John, inspired by God, penned a promise in his first epistle that sums up the truth about the unsurpassed power of faith and our utterly attainable victory over fear. John wrote that our faith is the victory that overcomes this world (1 John 5:4 ESV).

The simple truth that John clearly stated is that faith is completely capable of overcoming the whole of this fallen world. Faith is the means by which every difficulty, sin, and burden we face during our time here on this earth is entirely capable of being overcome, including fear.

Although fear and faith are perfectly opposed to one another, they share an eerie similarity at their core. Fear and faith both peer into the unseen future. The striking difference between them, however, is what we see there. Fear looks into the endless possibilities that the future may hold, and through a haze of darkness and despair, fear sees dire circumstances, unavoidable tragedy, potential pain, crushing grief, and inevitable heartache looming on the horizon of our lives.[1]

Faith, however, looks to the very same future, and through the illumination of God's promises to His children, faith sees the possibility of unimaginable treasures (1 Corinthians 2:9) that a heavenly Father who gives "good gifts" bestows on us (James 1:17) even in the midst of the worst circumstances that one might encounter in this life.

Faith sees unconditional love that knows no bounds and conquers all things (Romans 8:37–39), peace that surpasses all understanding and valiantly guards our hearts and minds (Philippians 4:7), and hope that anchors our very souls to the power and presence of an Almighty God in heaven (Hebrews 6:19).

Faith and fear are similar in nature but so completely opposed to one another that they are constantly at war in those of us who struggle with fear. Deep within our minds, fear and faith stand toe-to-toe as mortal enemies and battle for complete control over our thoughts and ultimately our lives.

Sadly, fear often emerges victorious, but that is not the way it has to be. Faith can overcome fear. Faith can become our victory, just as the apostle John wrote.

When fear wins the war for our thoughts, it is not because our faith is incapable. It is simply because our personal faith exists in a weakened and fragile state. That was the first lesson God taught me that fateful night when I wound up with a fortune cookie in one hand and my dusty Bible in the other.

My faith was weak, wounded from years of fighting against fear and the darkness of this world, without the benefit of the strength and nourishment that can only be found in the power and presence of God. My shallow, nearly nonexistent relationship with God had left my faith pitifully fragile compared to my overwhelming and seemingly all-powerful fear.

One thing I did remember from my Sunday school education was that faith isn't supposed to be fragile. Scripture describes faith as a shield that deflects the attacks of our enemy (Ephesians 6:16). I imagine it kind of like Captain America's invincible shield.

My shield of faith certainly wasn't invincible. I'm not even sure it was whole. The night I read that fortune cookie, I imagine that my shield of faith looked like a slice of Swiss cheese, and as much as I love Swiss cheese, it doesn't make a very good shield. It's far too hole-y.

The enemy's flaming arrows of fear sailed right through the very same holes in my faith that had been there, growing larger and larger since my early childhood when I had first encountered fear. They flew unhindered straight into my heart, my mind, and my soul, and that's exactly why I was paying the too great price of going through life afraid.

My faith was fractured, and for the first time in my life, due to the sudden clarity that always comes from hearing the voice of God, I knew it. With that knowledge, I became determined to fix my faith, making it more powerful than my fear, so I could experience the victory the apostle John promised was possible through faith.

Chapter 2

The Snare and the Snake

During the Great Depression, arguably one of the most fearful times in the history of America, President Franklin D. Roosevelt said, "The only thing we have to fear is fear itself—nameless, unreasoning, unjustified terror which paralyzes needed efforts to convert retreat into advance." Roosevelt spoke of fear as if it were, in and of itself, something to be feared, and I think he was on to something.

Fear seems simply a natural part of humanity, an emotion that is, in all likelihood, born in us the very moment we are born into this world in a flood of tears and screaming protest that everything we have known from the moment we were conceived has suddenly changed. For some of us, fear becomes something much more unnatural. For some, fear becomes a force of darkness that overwhelms, paralyzes, and even goes so far as to hold us in bondage (Hebrews 2:15).

It is as though fear becomes something more sinister than simply fear. Though Roosevelt grasped this concept, he seemed to have trouble putting a name to it. He described this fear as nameless. But God gave this fear a name in scripture that perfectly describes its potentially threatening nature. In the Old Testament book of Proverbs, King Solomon called fear a snare or a trap (Proverbs 29:25).

The Snare of Fear

I picture the snare of fear as a large, mouth-shaped, metal trap with sharp, needlelike teeth. It is always present in our lives, but the everyday routine and normalcy of our days usually hides it. It lies in wait until suddenly something on the path ahead of us strikes fear in our heart.

In that moment of fear, the trap is sprung, and we react in one of two ways: advance by wrapping ourselves in a shield of faith and stepping over the snare's iron jaws unscathed or become paralyzed, now caught in the clutches of that trap, a victim of its debilitating grip.

An example of how the snare of fear might work in a life consumed by fear is this: You're on your way to visit a sick friend to take her some soup and crackers because she is too sick to take care of herself, and you know that this is exactly the kind of thing that Jesus would like for you to do.

But out of the blue, you suddenly wonder if it's possible for you to contract the illness that has made your friend so deathly ill. Just for a second, you allow your mind to stroll down that dark path of wonder, and a million other questions begin to pop into your head as if on rapid fire from the depths of your imagination. *What if I catch what she has? What if it makes me sick? What if it makes me really, really sick? What if I become so sick that I can't take care of my own family? What if I die?*

In a very brief moment, a simple fearful thought escalates from something seemingly reasonable to something completely unlikely. Fear becomes the unreasoning, unjustified terror that Roosevelt spoke of. Of course, at the time, you don't see it that way. At that moment, it seems completely plausible, and you inadvertently fall victim to the snare of fear.

Before you know it, the needlelike teeth of fear tighten around your heart and mind, and suddenly the feat of dragging that heavy, burdensome trap to the bedside of a sick friend becomes a seemingly impossible task. You conveniently remember that you have something else that really needs to be done that day, something a little less frightening. Fear wins a victory, and that one small victory gives it strength.

The next time you face that same kind of fear, the snare snaps up even more quickly and powerfully onto your heart and mind and then even more so repeatedly until, before you even realize what's happening, you're bathing in Germ-X and avoiding any sickness at all cost because fear completely ensnares you. That's how the snare of fear works in our lives. It wins one small, seemingly insignificant battle. Then it wins another and another until our fear eventually begins to completely consume us.

To make matters worse, hundreds, perhaps thousands, of fears might rise up over the course of our lives. Each one has the potential to become a snare in our lives. Some of us struggle consistently with one or two traps while still living a fairly normal existence, while others become bound up by so many different fears that we end up living a completely defeated existence as slaves to our fears (2 Peter 2:19–20).

That's exactly the state I was in when I read the fortune out of the Chinese cookie about fear and faith. I was a prisoner in my own mind, so overwhelmed by fear and anxiety that I had become entirely incapable of completing some of the simplest tasks in life. I was completely ensnared by my fears, but over time, I came to realize that fear was not my true captor.

Fear is a snare, and snares do not exist on their own. They are set in our lives.

The Sneaky Snake

My family and I live in the middle of a cotton field. Needless to say, a little wildlife is around. I also live in a house full of boys, so occasionally I have the great pleasure of having grubby hands poking said wildlife—frogs, lizards, worms, and you get the picture—into my face. My boys have made pets of them all … all but snakes. (Thank the good Lord above!)

Unfortunately I do see snakes fairly regularly in my yard, my flower beds, and even my garage, but never in my house. (Again, thank the Lord!) I did find a lizard in my breakfast nook once, but I didn't really have to wonder how that got there.

Recently, however, my husband found a very large snakeskin underneath an old comfy chair in the office of his farm shop building. It is a chair I sit in quite often as I read or study while my husband tinkers in his shop, the same chair I'm sitting in as I write these words.

Since his discovery, I've wondered how many times I might have sat in this chair with a large snake curled up underneath it, unbeknownst to me. If I had known the snake were there, I certainly would never have gotten comfortable. In fact, I probably wouldn't have entered the room, much less sat in the chair.

Satan, our enemy in this world, is introduced in scripture as a serpent or snake and referred to as the most cunning of all the wild animals that the Lord had made (Genesis 3:1 HCSB). It's interesting to me that scripture shows Satan's first appearance not in hell or in the evils of the fallen world, but in the paradise of the garden of Eden, getting up close and personal with Eve.

Oftentimes we look for Satan in places we know he frequents, in the weeds of sin and rebellion, slithering along out in the darkness of the world, attacking others. We think we catch a glimpse of him every once in a while, and we either avoid him or grab a garden hoe and attack him, depending on how close he is to our home, our family, or our loved ones.

But I wonder how often Satan is curled up underneath our comfy chair, making himself at home, listening to our deepest secrets, or perhaps even whispering what-ifs to our subconscious. What if you get sick? What if you fail miserably? What if they don't like you?

How often do we hear his voice and fail to realize that it's him because we're in our comfy chair in our comfy office, and we don't expect him to be right there with us ... so very close?

Unfortunately our enemy in this world is close, and he is on the prowl. The apostle Peter warned us of this truth when he wrote, "Be serious! Be alert! Your adversary the Devil is prowling around like a roaring lion, looking for anyone he can devour" (1 Peter 5:8 HCSB). Peter said *anyone*. That includes you and me. No matter who we are or who we think we are, we all just look like lunch to him.

Not only is Satan seeking people to devour, he's looking for ways to devour them. For some, certain sins become weaknesses, and temptations become traps that keep them defeated. For others, anger is a snare that enslaves (Proverbs 22:24–25).

For still others, fear is the snare of choice in Satan's plot to devour. Fear may be a normal part of the human existence, but the snare of fear is not, and it does not stand alone in the life of a Christian. Our enemy in this world crafts the snare of fear early in our lives, and it is tailored to us. It is tested over the course of our lives and perfected every time it clamps around our hearts and minds.

A very clever snake sets the snare of fear in our lives. It may be difficult to think of Satan being so close to us that he can manipulate us on such a personal level. We really do hate to give him too much blame in our lives, but we must be careful not to give him too little.

Satan has been roaming this world for a very long time, since he showed up in the garden of Eden in the form of a snake looking to devour Eve. We cannot underestimate his understanding of the human condition or his ability to use that knowledge to entrap and ensnare even the children of God.

I believe that the snare of fear is one of the most powerful weapons in our enemy's arsenal in a large part because we fail to recognize that there may be such a sneaky snake behind the fear in our lives.

We don't want to believe that Satan could know us so intimately as to use our deepest, darkest fears against us. We don't want to believe that we are allowing our enemy in this world to toy with us and to manipulate us on such a personal level. We would much rather believe that there is just something wrong with us. Ironically, Satan would rather us believe that too. He prefers to operate in the shadows.

Furthermore, he knows that, the minute we realize how close he is and how much power we've allowed him to have in our lives, we will grab our garden hoe and begin to fight back. He also knows that, if we fight back, we will be victorious by the power of our faith. And that is exactly what we are going to do. We are going to fight back.

Simply Resist

Nowadays when I go to sit in the comfy chair in my husband's shop office to read, write, or study, I always take a quick peek underneath it, just to make sure a huge snake isn't curled up there.

Before we move any further in this journey, we should do that in our lives as well. Let's peek into our souls, peer down deep into our spirits, and begin to see the fear-filled attacks of Satan for what they are, traps and snares.

The very first step toward overcoming anything in this life is opening our eyes to the reality of the situation. Open your eyes now, and take a good, long look at the snare of fear in your life and the snake that uses that snare to his advantage.

Consider your deepest, darkest fear, whether it be rejection, death, or failure, and ask yourself if it has become a trap or a snare in your life. If your honest answer is yes, then it is not by chance that you are sitting in your comfy chair reading this book. Chances are, a snake is curled up there with you.

Fortunately for us, snakes are cowardly creatures, especially when they know they've already been beaten. James, the half-brother of Jesus, wrote, "Resist the devil and he will flee from you" (James 4:7). Simply resist.

It's time for us to grab our garden hoe and begin to fight. The slightest effort on our part through the power and presence of God will turn that roaring lion Peter wrote about into a frightened kitten and send our enemy fleeing with his tail tucked between his legs because even he knows that the victory belongs to us.

Chapter 3

Freedom from Fear

As we grab our garden hoe and begin to fight against the snare of fear and the snake behind that snare, the most important concept that we can possibly grasp is that, as children of God, we will never fight alone. Our heavenly Father will join us in our struggle against fear. Freedom from the snare of fear is gained in part through our attempts to escape from fear and partly through God's rescue of us from fear.

The apostle Peter explains this concept in 1 Peter 5. Immediately after warning us to be on the lookout for the roaring lion, Satan, and his efforts to trap us in his snares in order to devour us, Peter tells us to *stand firm* against him and *be strong* in our faith" (1 Peter 5:9 NLT, emphasis mine), which is our part. Then in the next verse, the apostle Peter tells us about our heavenly Father's part. He says that, in the midst of our attempt to stand firm and be strong, God will personally restore us, support us, strengthen us, and place us on a firm foundation of faith in Him (1 Peter 5:10 NLT).

These few scriptures are the basis for the remainder of our journey and are key to finding the freedom from fear that is possible through faith in our heavenly Father. Standing firm against Satan and his sinister snare involves holding our ground against fear and mentally preparing ourselves to move forward in faith. Being strong in our faith involves taking a good hard look at our personal faith and our own individual relationship with our heavenly Father so we might clearly see the weak areas in our shield of faith that are evidenced by our susceptibility to fear. And then we lean on God to help strengthen our faith in Him. In the fight against fear, our role is to stand firm and be strong in faith.

As we move forward in this journey and escape the snare of fear, we will dig into the apostle Peter's words in 1 Peter 5:9 and look at what it really means to stand firm against fear and be strong in our faith, but before we do that, let's take a quick look at our heavenly Father's role in this journey and the promise of rescue that He made through the apostle Peter in 1 Peter 5:10.

Never Alone

In the Old Testament, God offered the children of Israel a life of freedom in a breathtaking land of heaven on Earth. He broke the bonds of their slavery to Egypt, walked with them through the wilderness journey, and eventually enabled them to defeat their enemies and claim their Promised Land as a free nation. Near the end of the Old Testament, however, the Israelites, through their own poor choices, lost the freedom they had been given, and much of the nation was taken away as slaves to the kingdom of Babylon.

As the nation of Israel fell to the Babylonian empire, God spoke through the prophet Jeremiah about His captive children,

> I will keep My eyes on them for their good and
> will return them to this land. I will build them
> up and not demolish them; I will plant them and

not uproot them. I will give them a heart to know
Me, that I am Yahweh. They will be My people,
and I will be their God because they will return to
Me with all their heart (Jeremiah 24:6–7 HCSB).

As God watched His precious children waste away in a
Babylonian prison, He made plans for their good. He prepared
to eventually return them to the land He had given them. He
was determined to love them back to Himself and to restore their
freedom.

We are so like the children of Israel. Our heavenly Father
means for us to be free, but we find ourselves bound up in spiritual
chains of fear and worry. Our heavenly Father watches over us in
our struggle, and He sees us in the same merciful light that He
saw the children of Israel. No matter how far we may have fallen
to fear, God has His eyes turned toward us for our good. He longs
to build us up, to help us as we attempt to stand firm against fear
and be strong in our faith.

Our heavenly Father longs to intervene in our lives and help
us to live the life of spiritual freedom that He has planned for us.
He longs to help us overcome the power of the snare of fear and
the snake behind that snare. He longs to rescue us. Our heavenly
Father won't rescue us, however, from a struggle like the one
against fear until we make the first move and attempt to escape.

Our role in the journey before us is to stand firm and be
strong in our faith. That is how we will escape fear as we move
forward in later chapters. The path before us, however, is not an
easy one. As we move forward and fight against fear, there is no
doubt that we will find ourselves in the midst of a raging fire of
fear from time to time. That is the nature of the journey.

The beautiful part of the struggle we face is that, as we work
to escape, our heavenly Father will come alongside us and rescue

us in ways we never dreamed were possible. As we embark on this journey, it is absolutely imperative that we realize that we will never be alone.

God will join us in the midst of the fire, where we will find what we are looking for, freedom from fear.

Fiery Rescue

Three brave Hebrew slaves— Shadrach, Meshach, and Abednego—were among the Babylonian captives that God spoke so lovingly of through the prophet Jeremiah in the scriptures above. If you've spent any time in church, you've likely heard their story more than once.

Shadrach, Meshach, and Abednego stood firm against the threat of death in a fiery furnace as they refused to bow to the golden image of King Nebuchadnezzar on the plain of Dura. Their firm stance caused them to be thrown into the fiery furnace, but in the midst of the fire, Shadrach, Meshach, and Abednego gained freedom from their bondage by surviving King Nebuchadnezzar's fiery furnace in spectacular fashion. Scripture tells us that Shadrach, Meshach, and Abednego walked around in the midst of the fire, unharmed and free from their bondage (Daniel 3:25).

The part I love the most about the story of Shadrach, Meshach, and Abednego is that, when they stood in the midst of the fire, scripture tells us that they did not stand alone. A fourth man was walking in the furnace with them, one with an appearance like a son of the gods (Daniel 3:25). Their Savior and ours, Jesus Christ, joined the brave Israelite slaves in the fire. He will do the same for us.

Every single time we find ourselves in the midst of the fire— and we will find ourselves in the midst of a fiery furnace or two as we walk forward in this journey together and attempt to stand firm and strong in faith—Jesus will join us there. He will grab us by the right hand and help us as we walk straight through the heart of the fire (Isaiah 41:13).

In the midst of the fiery furnace, God performed a miracle for the three Israelite prisoners of King Nebuchadnezzar. He made them fireproof. Our heavenly Father desires to complete a miraculous work in our lives as well as He rescues us in the midst of our own fiery furnace. He will make us fearproof.

The Miraculous Work

The apostle Peter describes the miraculous work that we can expect to see our heavenly Father perform in our lives as we stand firm and strong in faith and experience our own fiery furnace of fear.

Peter assures us that, in the midst of our struggle against the roaring lion who is seeking to devour us, God will rescue us by restoring us, supporting us, strengthening us, and placing us on a firm foundation of faith in Him (1 Peter 5:10 NLT). The Greek words Peter used in his writing give insight into the nature of the miraculous work God completes in our lives when we walk through the fire of our fears with Him by our side.

First, Peter says God will restore us. The word *restore* means that God will mend what is broken in us.[2] Fear left undefeated in our lives breeds unbelief and distrust in our hearts. But as we seek to stand firm against fear, God will heal our broken, distrustful, fearful hearts. God will mend the brokenness in us and restore us to a more complete trust in Him.

Second, Peter says God will support us. The Greek word translated as *support* speaks to stabilizing and strengthening and is associated with the mind.[3] In our struggle with fear, we often become prisoners in our own minds, subject to attacks by our enemy that appear as fearful thoughts and wild imaginations, or what-ifs.

In the midst of panic attacks, I would pray for God to heal my body and my mind. Even in the depths of my own prison of fear, I realized that my fears were mostly in my own head and my mind needed a healing touch from God just as desperately as my panicked body did. Scripture promises that He will do that for us.

As we stand against fear, God will stabilize our minds. He will also stabilize and support our imaginations and help us to rest our thoughts on our faith and not our fear. Our heavenly Father will give us a peace that surpasses all understanding for our war-torn minds (Philippians 4:7).

Third, Peter promises that God will strengthen us. The Greek word translated as *strengthen* means exactly that, but just as the word support is associated with the mind, the word *strengthen* is associated with the soul.[4]

This promise speaks to God's strengthening of our innermost being. Our soul is the part of us that makes us who we are, the person that God created us to be. It is the piece of eternity that God placed within our hearts the moment we were conceived (Ecclesiastes 3:11). Our soul is unique to us. As we seek to stand firm against fear, God will strengthen the very core of our being with hope. He will bind us to eternity with an anchor of hope and whisper strength into our souls (Hebrews 6:19).

Finally, Peter promised that God would place us on a firm foundation. The Greek word used here—and the root word it is derived from—speaks to the act of laying a firm foundation. It speaks to new beginnings.[5]

This is the promise of a new beginning in our lives. Scripture promises that God will give us a fresh start on a firm foundation of faith as we seek to stand firm. He will not leave us in the darkness of fear. Our Father will rescue us.

As we move forward in this journey toward the inevitable fire and divine rescue that takes place in the flames, the words that God told the prophet Isaiah to say to those with fearful hearts seem fitting, "Be strong, and do not fear, for your God is coming to destroy your enemies. He is coming to save you" (Isaiah 35:4 NLT).

He is coming to rescue you from the snare of fear. All you have to do is move forward in faith even when the path ahead takes you through the fire because "you will not be scorched when you walk through the fire, and the flame will not burn you" (Isaiah 43:2 HCSB). Instead, in the midst of the raging fire, you will gain freedom from fear and become fearproof.

Stand Firm— Foundations of Faith

Chapter 4

Stand Firm

Our goal for the journey before us is to become free from the snare of fear. Becoming free from the snare of fear in our lives, of course, doesn't mean that we will never again feel fear. Fear is a natural part of our humanity, and it will rise up in our lives. Learning how to react when fear threatens to overwhelm us is the key to cultivating a faith that overcomes our fear and sets us free from the snare of fear.

In 1 Peter 5, the apostle Peter tells us exactly how to react to the roaring lion's efforts to trap us in the snare of fear. Immediately after warning us to be on the lookout for Satan, Peter tells us to *stand firm* against him and *be strong* in our faith (1 Peter 5:9 NLT, emphasis mine).

As noted in the last chapter, this scripture is the basis for all that we will attempt to accomplish as we move forward in our fight against fear, to stand firm and be strong in faith. For the time being, however, we're going to concentrate on the first half of Peter's instruction, where he tells us to stand firm.

Standing firm against Satan and his sinister snare of fear is the first step toward our goal of overcoming fear. Standing firm simply means holding our ground. When we stand firm in moments of fear, we mentally prepare ourselves to move forward in faith and simultaneously refuse to fall backward in fear.

Every Christian is capable of standing firm in the face of fear because of what we, as Christians, stand on, a solid foundation of faith in our heavenly Father. I probably didn't have to tell you that. Most Christians know intellectually that we have a foundation of faith in God on which we are supposed to be able to stand firm. Unfortunately that knowledge doesn't always keep us from losing our footing and falling down to fear anyway. Fear has a tendency to cause us to completely forget about the foundation of faith that rests beneath our feet.

The key to standing firm is remembering the solid foundation of faith beneath our feet in moments of fear so we can focus on our faith instead of the fear that is rising up against us and threatening to overwhelm us.

As we move forward in this journey, we will guard against our forgetfulness and steady our stance by identifying two simple yet memorable footholds that represent a sure and solid foundation upon which we can stand firm against any fear at any time in our lives.

These two footholds can be seen clearly in the same story we've already briefly looked at, the story of three Israelite slaves who stood firm at a time when fear could easily have overwhelmed their hearts and caused them to very literally bow down to their fear and their captor.

Footholds

Shadrach, Meshach, and Abednego were among the many young, intelligent men brought to Babylon during the fall of Israel near the end of the Old Testament. Because of their desirable qualities, they were made slaves to King Nebuchadnezzar.

Their first appearance in scripture is in Daniel 1, when they, along with Daniel, desired to abstain from certain foods and obey God's instructions to their people regarding their diet. We learn from this first mention of Shadrach, Meshach, and Abednego that these men were not half-hearted in their faith. They clung to their faith and their God, even in the midst of the very worst circumstances.

Later in the book of Daniel, when their Babylonian captor commanded these same three men to bow down to a golden image that he had set up as a god on the plain of Dura, they refused. That's when their situation got really sticky, and, no doubt, fearful.

They were pulled from the crowd of worshippers and brought before King Nebuchadnezzar so he might personally frighten some obedience into them, but though he had defeated the entire nation of Israel, King Nebuchadnezzar could not defeat the spirit of these three slaves. They were already being obedient, just not to him. They were obeying their heavenly Father.

King Nebuchadnezzar tried to scare Shadrach, Meshach, and Abednego into submission. He offered them one final chance to bow down to his image, and then he threatened them with an unthinkable death in a fiery furnace if they refused again.

As he discussed his terms with the three Israelite slaves, King Nebuchadnezzar asked them the question, "What god will be able to rescue you from my power?" (Daniel 3:15).

Unfortunately for King Nebuchadnezzar, Shadrach, Meshach, and Abednego knew a God who was able, and even worse for the king, they believed that their God would rescue them from his power. They told King Nebuchadnezzar just that as they stood firm before him and refused, yet again, to bow down.

Shadrach, Meshach, and Abednego, in reply to King Nebuchadnezzar's cutting question, defiantly answered, "The

God whom we serve is *able* to save us, and He *will* rescue us from your power" (Daniel 3:17, emphasis mine).

In a moment when fear could easily have caused them to forget all about their faith in favor of an easier and much less intimidating path, Shadrach, Meshach, and Abednego remembered two very important and yet simple truths about their God that became footholds beneath their feet and enabled them to stand firm against their captor. God is able, and He will.

First, Shadrach, Meshach, and Abednego told King Nebuchadnezzar in direct rebuttal to his question, "If we are thrown into the blazing furnace, the God whom we serve is *able* to save us" (Daniel 3:17 NLT, emphasis mine).

They were absolutely correct. The truth is that God is able to save each one of us from any fearful situation that we face in our lives. Shadrach, Meshach, and Abednego knew that. They knew their God could save them from the fiery furnace of King Nebuchadnezzar. They knew that, in His power, He could even allow them to endure the blaze of the furnace unharmed. So instead of bowing down to fear and the golden image of their captor, they choose to focus on God's ability to work in their fearful situation.

But they didn't stop there. With their very next breath, Shadrach, Meshach, and Abednego told King Nebuchadnezzar, "He *will* rescue us from your power, Your Majesty" (Daniel 3:17 NLT, emphasis mine).

In the face of certain death, the Israelite slaves proclaimed aloud their belief that God would intervene in their fearful situation. They knew the Lord had rescued their people from the iron-smelting furnace of Egypt in order to make them His very own people (Deuteronomy 4:20), and they believed that He would rescue them from Babylon as well.

God had promised the children of Israel over and over through the Old Testament prophets that He would rescue them from the hand of their enemies, and Shadrach, Meshach, and Abednego believed that He would rescue them from the hand of King Nebuchadnezzar. They believed that God would act in their fearful situation, and they told King Nebuchadnezzar just that.

These three Israelite slaves were able to stand firm against their captor and the power of fear in their lives by planting one foot on the foundation of what they knew God could do in their situation and the other foot on a foundation of what they believed God would do. We can do the same by simply remembering in moments of fear that God can and will rescue us as well.

The First Stance

The psalmist wrote, "My eyes are ever on the Lord, for only he will release my feet from the snare" (Psalm 25:15 NIV).

In order to find freedom from the snare of fear in our lives, we must learn to shift our gaze away from our fear and toward the only one who can and will rescue us from every fearful situation in our lives, our heavenly Father.

When we focus on God's ability to act in our lives and His willingness to do just that, we put two footholds beneath our feet that can instantly become a foundation of faith on which we are able to stand firm as we expectantly await His rescue of us.

And He will rescue us. God always rescues his children. He may not always rescue us the way we think He should – I doubt Shadrach, Meshach, and Abednego really thought that walking around in King Nebuchadnezzar's fiery furnace unharmed would be God's method of rescue for them—but He will always rescue us when we turn to Him for help in our own fearful situations. And those of us who struggle with fear need to be rescued regularly.

I have not spent one day of my life in physical captivity, yet I can't help but think that, even as slaves, Shadrach, Meshach, and Abednego were more free, spiritually speaking, than I have been for much of my life. I have spent so much of my life bowing down to panic and worry, falling to the ground in the face of terror and dread.

It's almost startling to think that standing firm in the face of fear could be as simple as remembering God's ability and willingness to work in my own fearful situations and learning to shift my focus to that, but it really is just that simple for us. The difficult part is all His.

We'll spend the next two chapters looking at simple strategies to help us remember God's ability and willingness to intervene in our fearful circumstances on our behalf as we seek to stand firm in the face of fear. After that, we'll delve into the second part of Peter's instruction to us, to be strong in faith.

Chapter 5

God Is Able to ...

My oldest son was born nine weeks premature. It was a wonder that either of us survived the difficult pregnancy that brought him into this world, but after only a few weeks in the Neonatal Intensive Care Unit (NICU), TJ was deemed well enough to go home.

Aside from his small size and a portable heart monitor that remained attached to him, he appeared to be progressing as any newborn should. The Saturday after we arrived home, however, my husband and I were awakened in the early hours of the day to the sound of the alarm on TJ's heart monitor alerting us to a low heart rate. As soon as I picked him up, the noise stopped, and he appeared fine, but the monitor continued to alarm sporadically throughout the morning, so we decided to take him to a nearby hospital.

The doctor there performed a number of tests and found nothing wrong, but out of an abundance of caution, he sent us by ambulance to a children's hospital a little further down the road. An hour and a half later, TJ and I emerged from the back of an ambulance at Le Bonheur Children's Hospital in Memphis.

A very few moments after our arrival, I stood in a small room and watched as my baby boy turned a grayish-blue color and stop breathing entirely. The monitors they had hastily attached to him loudly proclaimed his lack of life, and the only other person in the room, a nurse, yelled loudly for help as she searched frantically for a mask small enough to fit his tiny face and allow her to force air into his lungs as she performed CPR. There was no such mask to be found, so she cupped her hand over his tiny face and improvised.

TJ was unnaturally cold and a deathly grey, and the only sign of life in him was a sporadic heartbeat that ever so slowly returned as the nurse forced air into his lungs and then gently pumped his tiny chest with her fingers. Suddenly a host of doctors and nurses appeared from nowhere, and the decision was made to put TJ on a ventilator while they determined what exactly had caused his frail body to give up life.

My husband, who had arrived in a separate vehicle, and I watched as a doctor attempted to insert a tiny tube into TJ's airway. The first attempt failed. They forced more air into his lungs, and the doctor tried a second time, another failure. A third attempt, a fourth, and then a fifth all failed.

By that time, the doctor was visibly upset. Her eyes met mine, and I could see the panic in them as she whispered to those nearest her that TJ's airway was beginning to swell shut from her attempts to intubate him and save his life.

Watching the scene unfold, a nurse gently took me by the hand and led me out of the room and into a busy hallway. I let her. I knew she didn't want me to watch my son die, and I didn't know if I could.

People continued to rush in and out of the room, and a certain doctor was called to the ER over the hospital's intercom system. Dr. Kevin Brinkman got the endotracheal tube into my son's airway on the ninth attempt. I have never forgotten that doctor's name, and it would be easy for me to look at him as my son's savior, but I know better.

I saw the look in the doctor's eyes that day. A woman, who had, no doubt, witnessed death on many occasions as an ER doctor, believed she was witnessing it again that day, even as she struggled to save my son. She couldn't save him, but God could.

And He did. The Master Physician rescued my son that day when He guided Dr. Brinkman's skilled hand. He ordered our steps all that day. He got us to the ER at Le Bonheur just in time, mere moments before my son coded, by prompting the first doctor to send us to a children's hospital in spite of the fact that he had found nothing wrong.

God kept his hand on my son that fateful day, just as he had done throughout my difficult pregnancy and the heart-wrenching weeks after his birth. TJ's survival was nothing short of a miracle.

Remember When

God can perform miracles, make the impossible possible, turn water into wine, heal the sick and raise the dead, persuade the wicked to accomplish His will, and prompt the righteous to do the same. He can move the stars in the heavens and mountains on this earth, both literally and figuratively. We all know that God's abilities are endless.

Yet in moments of fear and worry, we tend to forget everything we know about our heavenly Father and His ability. And our forgetfulness allows our fear to run rampant. If we would remember God's ability in moments of fear, we would begin to stand a fighting chance against our fears.

I learned this lesson for myself in the early years of TJ's life. His first few years included many, many trips to emergency rooms. His premature birth and the lung condition he was born with haunted him for a long time, but every time I lay in a hospital bed cradling my son in my arms as he struggled to breathe, I remembered what God had already done in his life.

Even in the face of a mother's worry, when I remembered that terrible, wonderful day when TJ coded in the Le Bonheur ER, I was reminded that God could rescue my son again if the need arose, and I found a measure of peace. I learned to rest on God's ability instead of worrying myself sick about circumstances I had no power over.

It wasn't until later that I realized this is exactly what scripture teaches us to do. In the Old Testament, God performed countless miracles for the children of Israel, and then He encouraged them in scripture to remember what He had done for them in the past so they would trust Him for their future (Psalm 105:5).

He instructed the Israelites to set up festivals, monuments, and numerous traditions specifically designed to remind the people of the miracles that He had already performed for them so they would continue to look to Him for provision in times of worry and need.

God taught the children of Israel in scripture that they could stand firm on a foundation of faith in His ability, a stance Shadrach, Meshach, and Abednego exemplified during their encounter with King Nebuchadnezzar on the plain of Dura.

We can do the same thing. We can learn to focus on God's ability in all our fearful situations, simply by remembering what He has done in the past. It doesn't even have to be our past. If you don't have a story like the one above, it doesn't matter. There are countless testaments to God's ability all around us. We just have to open our eyes and look for them. When we do—and when we look at what God has done in the past—we get a clear vision of

His ability to act in our present circumstances, no matter how fearful they may be.

God Is Able to Give Life in the Face of Death

I had a friend who was diagnosed with late-stage cancer several years ago. At the time, doctors told her that she had only a few months to live. Her faith in God's ability didn't waver for a moment. Other believers prayed with her constantly throughout the rest of her life, and she lived for more than three years.

I visited with her shortly before her passing, and even in the very face of death, she proclaimed the miracle of prolonged life that God had gifted her with. She was grateful for every precious moment that she was able to share with her family, especially her children.

Scripture tells a similar story. Shortly after a glorious victory by God in his life, Judah's King Hezekiah became deathly ill. The prophet Isaiah came to him and told him to set his affairs in order because his illness would lead to death. Unwilling to accept this untimely death, Hezekiah immediately cried out to God in prayer, asking Him to give him more time (2 Kings 20:1–3).

Isaiah heard from God a second time and returned to Hezekiah. This time he told the king that his sickness would last for three days, and in the end, God would add fifteen years to his life. Just like my friend, God gave King Hezekiah the miracle of a prolonged life (2 Kings 20:4–6).

When we face health concerns that are well beyond our control, we can remember these stories and others like them and focus on God's ability to give the miracle of life even in the face of certain death.

God Is Able to Heal

My nephew, Harrison, was born with two major heart defects. The first was life-threatening and required surgery within the first week of his life. My brother and his wife knew that God could rescue their son, and they asked Him for a miracle. Harrison sailed through the initial surgery and quickly began to thrive.

The second birth defect was a large hole in the wall of his heart. Originally the doctors left it alone in hopes that it would eventually heal on its own. They monitored his condition annually, and they eventually became increasingly certain that he would need to undergo a second surgery.

Over the course of the next year and after countless prayers, however, the hole closed completely with no surgical intervention, at least that's what the doctors said. Mending broken hearts is another one of God's abilities.

Scripture tells us that Jesus healed various diseases (Mark 1:34) during his ministry on this earth. He healed the lame (Matthew 21:14), the blind (Matthew 8:27–29), the mute (Matthew 9:33), and even the dead (Mark 5:41).

Jesus healed a mother's broken heart and raised a young man's dead body all in one fell swoop when he came upon a funeral procession in Nain (Luke 7:11–17). A leper once said to Jesus, "Lord, if You are willing, you *can* make me clean" (Matthew 8:1–3 NKJV, emphasis mine). Jesus did just that, and He still can today.

When worry threatens to overwhelm us, we can focus on what we remember about God's ability to heal broken bodies and mend broken hearts.

God Is Able to Calm Storms

Not long ago, I said good-bye to my husband and watched him leave for work. I walked around our yard for a moment, looking at a dark sky that had appeared out of nowhere, and then I headed inside. Almost immediately, my phone rang, and I was surprised to see it was my husband.

The tone of his voice was dramatically different than it had been only a few minutes before as he practically shouted through the phone, "I can see a tornado on the ground just off the highway. It's headed straight toward the house. You need to get into the storm shelter now!"

Quickly my boys and I climbed down into the shelter, and almost immediately I heard the roar of rushing winds. A moment later, after the noise died down, I climbed out of the shelter.

Almost as soon as I walked outside, I watched a tornado drop down out of the sky in the cotton field just behind my home. In awe, I watched as it moved away, meandering through the fields toward the ditch that runs behind our home.

My home stood completely unharmed, but I knew the storm that held the tornado had just passed directly overhead. The only explanation for the state of my home was that the storm had calmed as it passed over my home and family.

Scripture tells of a storm at sea that threatened to capsize a boat that Jesus and his disciples were traveling in. Jesus was asleep in the belly of the boat, but as the disciples grew terrified, they woke him, exclaiming, "Master, Master, we're going to drown!" Jesus simply rebuked the wind, and the storm ceased. Scripture says, "All was calm" (Luke 8:24 NLT).

When the winds of anxiety rage around us, we can remember God's ability to calm all the storms of our lives, both literal and figurative, and focus on that.

God Is Able to Change Lives

For more than fifteen years, my family and I watched as a person who was very dear to us struggled with a drug addiction. Several years ago, as this person sat in a jail cell, we decided to bind together, not in worry or frustration, but in prayer and fasting with a spirit of hope.

We believed that God could deliver this dear person from an addiction that seemed impossible to defeat. The experience was a powerful one. Over the course of a few weeks, we prayed and fasted together several times. Then we watched in awe as God performed a miracle. This dear person became a clean and sober witness of our heavenly Father's life-altering ability.

In the city of Jericho, Jesus encountered a rich tax collector, Zacchaeus. Though he had lived his entire life cheating others, changed by the touch of a Savior, the man declared on that day that he would give half of his wealth to the poor and pay back those he had wronged fourfold (Luke 19:1–8).

On the road to Damascus, Jesus encountered another man, one who had ravaged the church (Acts 8:3), thrown many early Christians into jail (Acts 8:3), and stood by, watching in approval, as a throng of Jews stoned the very first Christian martyr.

God changed the man's name from Saul to Paul, and He changed his heart as well. In a moment of revelation, the apostle Paul went from tearing down the early church to building up churches from nothing in numerous cities throughout the region.

In another dramatic turn of events, King Nebuchadnezzar, the same king who persecuted Shadrach, Meshach, and Abednego for failing to worship his god, learned to worship their God. The last words we see from Babylon's King Nebuchadnezzar in scripture are, "Now I, Nebuchadnezzar, praise and glorify and honor the King of heaven. All his acts are just and true, and he is able to humble the proud" (Daniel 4:37 NLT).

When circumstances seem absolutely impossible, we can remember that God can change lives and focus on His ability to make the impossible possible.

Imagine That

The list of things that God can do is endless. Scriptures gives enough examples of the wondrous works of God to fill sixty-six books. He has performed enough miracles in the lives of His followers to fill thousands more. They fill the shelves of bookstores all over the world.

Chances are, for any fear we face, we can find the story of a miracle that God has already performed to help us focus on His ability in our own situation. But if we can't, we can simply use our imagination.

Generally speaking, fear is based in speculation and imagination, and faith is based in truth. But this is one area of our faith where we can feel free to use our imagination. God is not limited in the future by what He has done in the past. Neither is He hindered by our limited imaginations. God can do anything that we can possibly imagine, and so much more. Scripture says that God is able to accomplish infinitely more than we might ask or think (Ephesians 3:20 NLT).

We can and should look to the past for examples of God's wondrous works, but we should never limit Him by what he's done in the past or even by what we can imagine is possible in a given situation. God is the master of miracles, and when the odds seem stacked against His children, He dearly loves to show out.

Perhaps the apostle Paul said it best in his letter to the church at Corinth, "No eye has seen, no ear has heard, and no mind has imagined what God has prepared for those who love him" (1 Corinthians 2:9 NLT).

We cannot even begin to imagine all that God is able to do in our own frightening situations, but in the face of our fear, worry, and anxiety, we should definitely try so we can focus on what is possible through His awesome power at work in our lives.

Reminding Ourselves

Focusing on what God is able to do in the fearful situations of our lives is a solid first step toward overcoming fear, and it really is a simple step in a lot of ways. But when we find ourselves in the middle of a raging fire of fear, it sometimes seems like it is much easier for us to forget what we know about God's ability than to remember to focus on it. We must guard against our natural tendency to forget.

Near the end of his life, Moses, knowing they would soon march into battle against their enemies and take the Promised Land, instructed the children of Israel to watch out and be careful never to forget what they had already seen God do, His ability. He urged them, "Do not let these memories escape from your mind as long as you live!" (Deuteronomy 4:9 NLT). As we begin to battle against our fears, we too must be careful never to forget, to never let the memories of God's ability to escape from our minds as long as we live.

Moses knew that the children of Israel, like us, would have trouble remembering. Throughout the book of Deuteronomy, nearly thirty times, he told the Israelites to remember, or not to forget. He even gave them a simple strategy to guard against their forgetfulness.

Moses encouraged the children of Israel twice to hide the words of God that he was sharing with them in their hearts. He told them to bind them as a sign on their hands and a symbol on their foreheads, to teach them to their children, and to speak of them at home and on the road, in the morning, and at night (Deuteronomy 11:18–20, 6:9).

The best way to remember God's ability and guard against our forgetfulness in moments of fear is to remind ourselves as often as possible of God's mighty works at home, on the road, in the morning, and at night.

This strategy can be as simple as availing ourselves daily of a few of the thousands of stories found in scripture that speak to God's ability, regularly listening to pastors and teachers, attending Bible studies, and reading devotionals.

Perhaps the most powerful way to remind ourselves of God's ability is to fellowship regularly with other believers, listening to the testimonies of what God has done in their lives and sharing our own. There are countless ways for us to remind ourselves of God's ability. It's important for us to choose strategies that work for us individually.

We will discover that, when we continually remind ourselves of God's ability, we will find it so much easier to remember His ability in moments of fear and to focus on His power to act in our fearful situations instead of focusing on our fears.

When we pour stories like the ones above, which highlight God's ability, into our hearts on a regular basis, when worry rises up in our everyday lives, memories of God's ability will already be at the forefront of our minds, ready for us to focus on. These memories will enable us to stand firm on our faith in God's ability to act in our fearful circumstances.

The more we hear, see, and know about our heavenly Father's ability, the more likely we'll be to remember Him and His ability when fear strikes. And that's exactly what we need to do in order to overcome fear in our lives. In every fearful situation we face, if we'll remember to rest our thoughts on God and His ability, we will take the first step toward standing firm against our fears.

Chapter 6

God Will ...

If remembering God's ability to act in our fearful circumstances is the first step toward standing firm against fear, then the second step is believing that He is willing to act on our behalf in the midst of all the fearful circumstances in our lives. This second step in our firm stance has the potential to make us immovable because it is based entirely on the unshakable truth of God's Word.

In order to stand firm against our fears as the apostle Peter instructed us, we will plant our first foot on our knowledge of God's ability and our second foot on our belief in God's promises to us, which tell us exactly what He will do in the fearful circumstances of our lives.

The promises of God fill scripture. In fact, it's interesting to note that nearly every time the phrase "fear not" appears in scripture, some sort of an explanation, or reasoning (promise), follows that speaks to exactly why we, as God's children, should not fear.

We can think of these promises in scripture as solid rocks of God's unlimited wisdom that become an unshakable foundation beneath our feet as we learn to stand firm upon them.

Scriptural Promises

Every promise found in scripture can be used to replace fear with faith, directly countering the whispered what-ifs of Satan and changing them to what-wills based on the unwavering truth of God's Word.

Fear can ask, "What if I die from the cancer invading my body?" We can stand firm on God's promise that He *will* determine whether we live or die (Deuteronomy 32:39, emphasis mine), not the cancer. Fear can ask, "What if I fail in my calling from Him?" We can stand firm on God's promise that He *will* enable us to do all things (Philippians 4:13, emphasis mine). Fear can ask, "What if I wind up rejected and alone?" We can stand firm on God's promise that He *will* never leave us nor forsake us (Deuteronomy 31:6, emphasis mine).

This is exactly what God intends for us to do with the promises made in scripture to us, use them as a foundation of faith to stand firm upon in the midst of the fearful circumstances of our lives.

The writer of Hebrews described this concept, "For He Himself has said, 'I will never leave you nor forsake you.' *So* we may boldly say: The Lord is my helper; I will not fear" (Hebrews 13:5–6 NKJV, emphasis mine).

The writer of Hebrews referred to the earlier written scripture of Deuteronomy 31:6 when God promised the Israelites that He would never leave them or forsake them. Then he explained that God breathed those words onto the pages of scripture so that we, even as His adopted children thousands of years later, could use them as a foundation of faith beneath our feet, enabling us to boldly proclaim God's promise of faithfulness over our own lives in the face of fear.

In other words, God promised that He would never leave us so we could, in midst of fearful circumstances, boldly proclaim that God is walking with us and that He is willing to help us. As we learn to do stand firm on God's promises to us, we can find the freedom from fear that we desperately need.

It is exactly what Shadrach, Meshach, and Abednego did in their own fearful circumstance when they said to King Nebuchadnezzar, "He (the God whom we serve) *will* rescue us from your power, Your Majesty" (Daniel 3:17, emphasis mine).

It is exactly what we will begin to do in our own fight against fear. We will stand firm on God's promises to us.

Personal Promises

Scripture contains hundreds of promises that can be used to specifically combat every fear or worry a person will ever face in this life, but as I learned to wage war against my own fears, I desired more personal promises, like the intimate promises God made to His children in scripture.

I desired to hear God speak to my specific fearful situations, and as I sought an intimate dialog with Him, I soon found that God desired to speak personal promises to me just as much as I desired to hear them.

Within the scriptures we've already looked at a few times, the apostle Peter promised us that God would become personally involved in our struggles and He would place us on a firm foundation (1 Peter 5:10). I believe that His personal involvement in our struggle against fear includes making very personal promises to our hearts and minds that can become a firm foundation beneath our feet.

God has always longed for close, intimate relationships with His children. He desires to speak personally to us. He has demonstrated that desire since the beginning of time when He visited Adam and Eve in cool of the day in the garden of Eden (Genesis 3:8) and countless times since.

The very first time the phrase "fear not" appears in scripture, God speaks it to His child, Abram, whom He later called Abraham. God told him, "Fear Not Abram: I am thy shield, and thy exceeding great reward" (Genesis 15:1 KJV).

God told Abraham that He would be his shield to protect him and his reward to bless him because He knew that Abraham would need that personal assurance to live the life that God had called him to live. God called Abraham to lead a fearful life. He had commissioned him to be the father of the nation of Israel, and He had instructed him to leave his family behind and travel to a distant land controlled by pagan kings.

During his lifetime, God led Abraham into many frightening situations, but He also spoke personally to him in the midst of those situations. He gave him a firm foundation of personal promises to stand upon in the face of his fears, even though we clearly see in scripture that Abraham didn't always stand on them. In Abraham's life alone, we can see God's desire to personally reassure and encourage His children in the face of their fears, but that is certainly not the only example we have.

God spoke to Isaac in a situation that could easily have sent him into a tailspin of worry. When neighboring peoples claimed the wells he had dug for his own herds, God told him, "Do not be afraid, for I am with you and *will* bless you. I *will* multiply your descendants, and they will become a great nation" (Genesis 26:24 NLT, emphasis mine).

When God called Jacob to turn his life upside down by leaving his home in his old age and traveling to Egypt, He spoke to him, "Do not be afraid to go down to Egypt, for there I *will* make your family into a great nation" (Genesis 46:3 NLT, emphasis mine).

As the king of Bashan was attacking Moses in battle, God said, "Do not be afraid of him, for I *have* handed him over to you, along with all his people and his land" (Numbers 21:34 KJV, emphasis mine).

To Joshua, who led the children of Israel on a fearful trek out of the wilderness and into the Promised Land, God spoke many personal promises. Once as he prepared for battle, God said, "Do not be afraid of them, for I *have* handed them over to you. Not one of them will be able to stand against you" (Joshua 10:8 HCSB, emphasis mine). God enabled Joshua to stand firm and fearlessly against his enemies by assuring him with a personal promise that none of his enemies would be able to stand against him.

Scripture is full of examples where God encouraged His children in situations where they could easily be overcome with fear by telling them what He would do in their lives so they could stand firm in the very face of their fears.

Over and over, we see these personal encounters between God and His children that assure us that He desires to have personal encounters with us as well. God desires to speak to each one of His children personally, through His Spirit that resides in us as believers.

Scripture confirms this desire in a psalm filled with promises of rescue and protection for God's children. Near the end of the psalm, the Lord, speaking of His children, says, "When they call on me, I *will* answer" (Psalm 91:15, emphasis mine).

Jesus confirmed this desire for conversation as well when He promised that, after His ascension, the Holy Spirit would, in His physical absence, speak to us and tell us things to come (John 16:13). When we are faced with worrisome situations in our lives and we take them to God, He will speak to us. He will personally tell us what He will do in our lives.

Through His Spirit, God will give us personal promises to enable us to stand firm on a foundation of faith and walk through this fearful world courageously. All we have to do is seek Him and His voice in our lives and learn to listen.

The Voice of God

God spoke to Moses through a burning bush (Exodus 3:2), to Daniel through the angel Gabriel (Daniel 8:16), and to the prophet Balaam through a donkey (Numbers 22:28). To the New Testament believers, however, God most often speaks through the soft whisper of the Holy Spirit within us.

During His time on earth, Jesus didn't just promise that the Holy Spirit would tell us things to come. He also gave us some insight into how the Holy Spirit will speak to us. He said, "When the Father sends the Advocate as my representative—that is, the Holy Spirit—he will teach you everything and will remind you of everything I have told you" (John 14:25–26 NLT).

Jesus promised His disciples and us that the Holy Spirit would continue speaking to us after He was gone, teaching us all things and reminding us of the words that He had already spoken. And that is exactly how God makes personal promises to us the majority of the time.

God whispers promises to us through the Holy Spirit as we read, study, or listen to the words of scripture. The Holy Spirit tells us personally what God will do in our specific situations using words that He has already spoken in scripture.

When I began to wage my own war against fear and to develop a more personal relationship with God, it didn't take long for Him to remind me of something I once knew, but had long since forgotten, was a part of His plan for my life, teaching. He led me to teach a Sunday school class at my church.

At the time, I felt like I was too young and inexperienced. I was afraid that I would say all the wrong things and fail miserably. Those around me, however, felt confident that I could fill the role, so I began to pray about my own fears regarding in the situation.

Within the next few days, in my quiet time with God, I happened upon His words to the prophet Jeremiah, "Do not say, "I am only a youth," for you will go to everyone I send you to and speak whatever I tell you. Do not be afraid of anyone, for I will be with you to deliver you (Jeremiah 1:7–8 HCSB).

As I sat cradling my Bible, God made that scripture personal to me through the ministry of the Holy Spirit. As only He can do, the Holy Spirit breathed life into the written words of scripture, and I heard Him whisper to my heart and mind, "You will speak whatever I tell you … do not be afraid … for I will be with you." God gave me a personal promise so I could stand firm against my anxiety in the matter.

In the months and even years that followed, every time my fear of failure threatened to keep me from teaching, even though I knew God had called me to do so, the Holy Spirit reminded me of that personal promise. And every time I taught, I knew that God was with me.

More often than not, God will use the words that He Himself personally breathed onto the pages of scripture (2 Timothy 3:16) to tell us what He will do in our lives. He will make scriptural promises into personal promises through our relationship with Him.

Though the vast majority of God's personal promises to us will come straight from the words of scripture, highlighting God's desire for us to spend time in His Word, sometimes God will whisper a promise within our hearts and minds during prayer and meditation.

Every once in a while, God will even speak to us completely out of the blue in an entirely unorthodox way. Remember my spiritual battle against fear began when I heard God speak to me through a fortune cookie. I've heard God whisper in the sunrise and in the darkest hours of the night. And, of course, He speaks regularly through preachers, teachers, and friends, and all our brothers and sisters in Christ.

One thing that we must always keep in mind is that God's personal promises, even if they don't come straight from scripture, will always line up with scripture. God's voice in our heart will never contradict His voice in the Bible.

The Voice of Truth

With the abundance of scriptures that speak to God's desire to communicate with His children, I believe God speaks to us much more often than we realize, but we fail to hear His voice. The still, small voice of our heavenly Father gets lost in the overwhelming barrage of worldly distractions.

We have to seek and really listen for God's voice in order to hear it in our lives. But it's not difficult. Seeking God's voice is as simple as developing and nurturing a personal relationship with Him. And developing a personal relationship with God is as simple as living life with Him. Regardless of how insignificant our worries and fears may seem in light of eternity, God wants to be involved in them because He wants to be involved in our lives.

True relationship is fostered in the everyday things of life. We call our friends or family members, those we are in relationship with, when we need comfort, assurance, or a voice of reason in our lives. There's nothing wrong with that, but God desires that we would do the same with Him. He wants us to share every part of our lives with Him so He can offer us comfort, assurance, wisdom, and insight as any true friend would.

Our heavenly Father wants us to run to Him in the midst of our fears, just as I used to run to my father in the middle of the night when the darkness overwhelmed me. He wants us to call on Him for advice and comfort, just like we do our friends and family. He wants us to search the pages of scripture for His wisdom so He can whisper to us, "Don't be afraid my child, for I will."

God desires for us to share the stuff of our life with Him and talk to him just as we would any other friend. Then as we watch and listen, He will respond, just as any other friend would.

As we begin to develop this kind of a personal relationship with God, we will begin to hear Him speak to the everyday situations of our lives. We will begin to hear Him tell us things to come through His Spirit living within us. God will share with us what He will do in our lives when we begin to purposefully share our lives with Him. Then He will help us to stand firm on those promises in the face of our fears.

As I have determined in my own heart to run to my heavenly Father in the midst of fearful circumstances, I have heard Him whisper many personal promises to my heart. And though His words to me haven't always been the ones I wanted to hear, they have always proven to be what I needed to hear. His is the voice of a true friend, one who speaks absolute truth with power and authority instead of the patronizing white lies that our earthly friends sometimes speak.

As we begin to seek God's voice in our lives, perhaps the most comforting thing for us to consider is that His promises are always based in truth. They have their foundation in certainty, not speculation. And they do not fail. That is exactly why His words can become a foundation beneath our feet and enable us to stand firm against fear.

Fearful thoughts are based on the what-ifs of Satan. But the personal promises of God are based on what will happen. And what will happen, for a God unrestrained by time, already has occurred. His promises are that certain.

In the scripture we glanced at earlier, God told Moses about the king of Bashan, "Fear him not: for I *have* delivered him into thy hand, and all his people, and his land (Numbers 21:34 KJV, emphasis mine). Notice that God didn't say "I will." Rather He said, "I have." When God spoke the word, it was already as good as done, and that is the way His promises work. When they are made, they are already completed in our lives. When God says He will, He already has.

God did the same thing when he told Joshua, "Do not be afraid of them, for I *have* handed them over to you" (Joshua 10:8 HCSB, emphasis mine). God told Joshua before he went to battle that He had already handed his enemies over to him.

When God does give us a personal promise, we can be absolutely certain that it will come to pass. Late in his life, Joshua testified to this fact, "None of the good promises the Lord had made to the house of Israel failed. Everything was fulfilled" (Joshua 21:45 HCSB).

All of the good promises that God made to Joshua and to all of the people of Israel came to pass. None of them failed. And not one of the personal promises God makes to you will fail either. When God tells you what He will do, you can rest assured He will do it.

We can stand firm against fear because of the certainty of God's promises to us.

Standing Firm

We can cut down the deceptive lies of fear, the teeth of Satan's snare, with the absolute truth of God's Word. That is exactly what the apostle Paul taught when he wrote, "We demolish arguments and every high-minded thing that is raised up against the knowledge of God, taking every thought captive to obey Christ" (2 Corinthians 10:4–5 HCSB).

Fearful thoughts are arguments raised up against the knowledge of God. We demolish these arguments when we turn the tables on fear and raise God's knowledge, that is, His promises of what He will do in our lives, up against the fearful thoughts and find that they have no choice but to obey. It is time for us to do just that, to step up onto the foundation of God's promises in our lives and begin to stand firm.

Start with the promises of scripture. More personal promises will come as you determine to seek God's voice in the everyday, worrisome situations of your life.

The promises of Isaiah 41 make a good foundation to begin to stand firm upon. "Do not fear, for I am with you; do not be afraid for I am your God. I will strengthen you; I will help you; I will hold on to you with My righteous right hand … I, the Lord your God, hold your right hand and say to you: Do not fear, I will help you" (Isaiah 41:10–13).

With the promises that God will strengthen you, help you, hold on to you, and even hold your right hand as He whispers to your heart, "Do not fear," you can place your feet on the firm foundation of God's promises in your own life and begin to stand firm against fear.

Standing firm in the face of fear is as simple as shifting our focus in moments of fear from the object of our fear to God's ability to act in our fearful circumstances and to God's promises to us, which tell us exactly what He will do in the fearful circumstances of our lives. But learning to stand firm is only the first half of our battle against fear.

Strong

in

Faith

Chapter 7

Be Strong

After telling us to stand firm against the roaring lion out to devour anyone and everyone he can get the steely sharp teeth of his many snares into, the second part of Peter's instruction for those of us fighting against the traps of our adversary is to be strong in our faith (1 Peter 5:9 NLT).

Our faith in God is meant to be an invincible shield to protect us from the traps of our enemy, and if it's not operating as such in our lives, there is a weak area in it, a hole in our shield. The truth of the matter is that, when the snare of fear—or any other snare of Satan, for that matter—becomes a problem in our lives, our personal faith is in need of some kind of strengthening.

Before we can hope to become strong in our faith, as Peter instructs us, we must first open our eyes to the weakness of our faith. We must come to understand for ourselves why our fear exceeds our faith at times and leaves us to pay the too great price of going through life afraid. We must identify the holes in our shield of faith that allow fear to penetrate deep into our hearts, our minds, and our souls.

Through my own struggle with fear and heartfelt desire to become strong in my faith as the apostle Peter instructed, I glimpsed three holes in my shield of faith through which the needlelike teeth of the snare of fear easily gained access to my heart, mind, and soul.

When I sought to mend those holes with my Father's help, I finally found some victory over fear in my life, and I know the same will be true for you because I believe that these same three holes are common to all who struggle with fear. Thankfully these holes can be mended.

Our faith can become the strong shield it is meant to be when we glimpse the holes that exist in it and allow our Father to mend them in ways that only He can.

Lack of Trust

The first and most comprehensive hole in our shield of faith is identified in the same scripture from which we learned that fear is a snare. King Solomon, arguably the wisest man in Old Testament literature, wrote, "The fear of man is a snare, but the one who trusts in the Lord is protected" (Proverbs 29:25 HCSB).

The first hole in our shield of faith is trust, or lack thereof. Trust is truly one of the most difficult things for us, as humans, to do wholeheartedly. No matter how much we might want to trust, we almost always hold back from a complete trust in anyone or anything, even God.

Unfortunately that lack, whether it is great or small in our own lives, makes us most susceptible to the snare of fear. The areas of our lives where we fail to trust God completely—our finances, our health, or our calling—are where we will struggle with fear and worry.

The truth is that every single fearful situation we face in life carries with it an opportunity to trust God with our whole heart. When we do trust Him completely, we become protected, or safe, not necessarily from the situation or the object of our fear, but from the anxiety, worry, or utter panic that the situation has the potential to breed in our lives.

When we trust, we become protected from the snare, and then we are able to face the fearful situation with a more positive outlook based on our faith instead of our fear and dread.

When we trust our heavenly Father we become fearless and faith-filled. On the other hand, when we fail to trust God, our shield of faith sports a dark hole where our trust ought to reside, in the shadowy corners of our heart where we hold back from a complete trust in God and His plan for our lives. And that dark hole becomes an easy access point for the teeth of the snare of fear.

As Christians, sometimes it's rather difficult for us to admit our struggle to trust God completely in our lives, but it truly is a struggle that is natural to our humanity. Rather than view this struggle as an area of shame, we can look at it as an opportunity for growth in our relationship with our heavenly Father, a place in our lives where our weakness can become His strength.

God desires to use our weakness to draw us nearer to Him and display his strength, if we'll simply allow it (2 Corinthians 12:9). As difficult as it may be, if we'll be completely honest with ourselves, we'll begin to see that every fight we've ever lost to fear reveals a trust-shaped hole in our faith.

Every fear that has the power to knock us off our feet, take our breath away, and cause us to bow down against our will can be traced to an issue of trust. If we pace the floors at night in worry over food, finances, or clothing, we are not trusting God to supply all our needs, as He has promised to do (Matthew 6:30–33).

If we are filled with anxiety at the thought of standing firm against those determined to tear us down, we aren't trusting God to stand with us (Deuteronomy 31:6). If health concerns cause panic to take us to the edge of reason, we aren't trusting God with authority over our life and our death (Revelation 1:18). If we are susceptible to the snare of fear in any way, we lack a complete trust in God and His plan for our lives.

Trust has the power to build a bridge over the snare of fear in our lives, allowing us to step over it unharmed, unshaken, and firm in our stance. We will concentrate on building that bridge in chapter eight. For now, we need to glimpse two more holes in our shield of faith.

Elusive Peace

In preparing His disciples for the hardships they would face after His imminent departure from them, Jesus promised that He would leave them—and us—with the gift of peace. "Peace I leave with you. My peace I give to you. I do not give to you as the world gives. Your heart must not be troubled or fearful" (John 14:27 HCSB).

To guard against fearful hearts, Jesus offers us the gift of His peace. But for those of us who have lived with fearful hearts for as long as we can remember, peace can seem very elusive in our lives and in our faith.

Anxious thoughts flood our minds even though we know that peace ought to rule there instead, making it much easier for us to see the second hole in our faith, peace, or lack thereof. The most important thing for us to understand about God's peace is that it is a gift, and like most gifts, it must be unwrapped. Some of us have a little more difficulty getting to the core of the gift than others, depending on our own life circumstances. It takes some of us a little longer to unwrap God's peace for ourselves.

The peace with God that we gain at the moment of our salvation is the origin of true peace in our lives. And that peace—God's peace—is meant to overflow into every fearful circumstance we face. Peace is meant to become an active part of our faith. When it doesn't—that is, when we lack God's peace in our lives—fear runs rampant. Fear easily penetrates our minds when the peace of God is not a functioning part of our faith, our shield.

We must learn to actively seek God's peace in all the fearful circumstance of our lives, unwrapping one of His most precious gifts to us, in order to win our own battle against fear. We'll do just that in chapter nine, but for now, we have one final hole to glimpse.

Hindered Hope

The writer of Hebrews, in a passage full of breathtaking imagery, calls our hope in Christ a sure and steadfast anchor of the soul that binds us to heaven (Hebrews 6:19).

For those of us who too often view our lives through a haze of fear, our hope seems to drown in the sea of uncertainty swirling around us on earth before it ever reaches heaven's crystal sea. Our temporal fears overwhelm our eternal hope, and our shield of faith pays the price with a third hole, lack of hope, that penetrates into the very core of our being, our soul.

Hope is similar to peace in that we usually realize when it's missing in our lives and our faith. We know the hole is there. We're just not sure how to fill it in. I believe the answer lies in the source, eternity.

Heaven is the source of all hope. Our hope begins in eternity and flows backward through time. We have hope in this life only because we have hope in the next. If we could learn to hope in heaven the way the heroes of faith in Hebrews 11 hoped, we would experience a strength of faith that cannot be found in any other way. We'll seek to do just that in chapter ten by anchoring ourselves to heaven by our hope.

Strong in Faith

It's no wonder that God is so adamant in scripture that we fear not. Fear directly counters the most fundamental desire of God's heart in respect to His children: that we would learn to trust Him in all things. On top of that, fear opposes two of the most precious gift associated with our salvation: our peace and our hope.

Of course, our heavenly Father desires for us to become strong in our faith and fearless. Perhaps that's why He gave us such a great example in the apostle Peter. You see, when the apostle Peter wrote that we should be strong in our faith, he was teaching a lesson that he had learned from experience.

We see in several scriptural accounts that, before Peter became the bold and courageous leader of the early church who wrote the hope-filled words, the same words we've looked to several times now, to the suffering saints, he himself struggled significantly with fear.

Peter's shield of faith was just as hole-y as ours early in his walk with Christ. In scripture, we see him terrified in the gospels, and then we watch in wonder as he becomes fearless in the book of Acts.

Peter's own faith was strengthened over time. And after his faith was strengthened, in an effort to strengthen the faith of others, as Jesus had personally instructed him to do (Luke 22:32), he wrote about a living hope (1 Peter 1:3), a gift of peace that grew with the knowledge of God (2 Peter 1:2), and an unfailing trust (1 Peter 2:6).

Early in his first letter, Peter wrote that, through our faith, God will protect us by His power until we reach heaven (1 Peter

1:5). Peter didn't call faith a shield the way the apostle Paul did, but he described it as such.

When he encouraged us to be strong in our faith, it was because he knew the power of faith. He had seen it in his own life. He had learned that faith protects us from the fiery darts of the wicked one, just as the apostle Paul described (Ephesians 6:16). Peter's faith became the invincible shield it was meant to be as he grew, learned, and drew ever closer to God.

Our faith can become a whole and invincible shield as well. When faith flourishes in our hearts as trust, in our minds as peace, and in our souls as hope, our faith will become the strong and invincible shield that it is meant to be in our lives.

Chapter 8

Getting to the Heart of Trust

"You put your right hand in! You put your right hand out! You put your right hand in, and you shake it all about! You do the hokey pokey, and your turn yourself around! That's what it's all about!"

Do you remember dancing the hokey pokey as a child? I do. I was an extremely shy child and more than a little awkward—terrified of rejection actually—but that never seemed to matter when I got wrapped up in the midst of the hokey pokey. All fear was lost. And I danced.

My favorite part was the very last verse. "You put your whole self in! You put your whole self out! You put your whole self in, and you shake it all about! You do the hokey pokey, and you turn yourself around! That's what it's all about!"

In that final verse of the hokey pokey, everyone really let loose and danced. We put our whole selves into the imaginary circle, and we shook everything from the tops of our heads to the tips of our toes. Even I, the shyest kid around, wholeheartedly danced with abandon. Since my days of dancing the hokey pokey, there have been very few things in life that I have been willing to give my whole self over to with such reckless abandon, even God.

I have sat on a church pew most of my life, sticking my right hand into the vast sea of Christianity, unwilling to dive into my faith with my whole self. And that is precisely why my faith has existed as a hole-y shield, powerless against my fear. A half-hearted faith produces a hole-y shield, and a hole-y shield just won't do in the fight against fear.

Even with one foot planted on the foundation of God's ability and the other on the foundation of God's promises, we desperately need our shield of faith to be whole and invincible so it can completely extinguish all the flaming arrows of the evil one.

We cannot afford to be half-hearted in our faith. We must dive into our faith with our whole selves and allow God to wash through the darkest depths of our hearts, our minds, and our souls so He can mend our shield of faith in ways that only He can.

In these final three chapters, we will focus on doing just that. We will take the first steps, and then we will rely on God to mend our hearts with trust, stabilize our minds with peace, and strengthen our souls with hope so we can stand firm on the foundation of faith that He Himself has already placed beneath our feet (1 Peter 5:10).

It's time for us to lower our own defenses and allow God access to our whole selves, beginning with our hearts, because it is within our hearts that we trust ... or fail to.

The Protected Heart

I remember my very first broken heart and the young man who broke it. I was seven and quite certain that I had found my soul mate living in a house just down the road. Unfortunately he didn't feel the same way, and he crushed my dreams of happily ever after when he broke my heart in two and proclaimed that he didn't want to be my boyfriend after all.

At some point in time, everyone experiences the pain of a broken heart. That pain is such that we only have to feel it once to become afraid of feeling it again. With our very first broken heart, we begin to teach ourselves to protect our hearts from the hurt that others can inflict on us. We're much more careful about giving our heart away a second time or third time and so on.

As we grow older and more completely understand the inherently sinful nature of humanity, those of us with fearful hearts often struggle to trust anyone with our fragile hearts. Even our closest family members and friends—our spouses, parents, and pastors—are feared untrustworthy.

We may desire to trust them. We may even tell ourselves that we do trust them. We certainly tell them that we trust them, but truth be told, we will bend over backward to keep our hearts protected even from those we are closest to in this life.

The lack of trust that we experience in our relationships with other people taints our relationship with God, and we do the same thing in our relationship with Him. We proclaim trust, but we don't truly trust Him with all our heart. And our fear wins.

We never give God enough of our heart to learn that He really is trustworthy. And because trust is the very heartbeat of our faith, our lack of trust deeply wounds our shield of faith, leaving it powerless against our fears.

In our very understandable, yet misguided, effort to protect our hearts from the hurt and pain of disappointment, we leave ourselves unprotected from the snare of fear and open to a different kind of pain, the pain of defeat.

In order to protect ourselves from the snare of fear (Proverbs 29:25), we must lower our own defenses and seek to trust in the Lord with all our heart (Proverbs 3:5), as the well-known proverb says.

Choosing to Trust

To trust someone is to believe in him or her. Even my young son had that figured out at an early age. I remember asking him what it meant to trust someone when he was about six, and I was really beginning to understand my own lack of trust in God.

He quickly answered, "It means you believe in someone. I believe in you, Mommy."

Oh, the awesome responsibility of motherhood!

TJ was right. To trust God is to believe in Him. When we trust God, we believe in His ability, which determines what He can do, and we believe in His character, which determines what He promises He will do.

We spent two chapters laying a firm foundation on which to place our feet based on God's ability and His promises, but that foundation won't ever do us any good if we don't believe in it.

If we don't truly believe that God can and will act in our lives, just as He promises to do, it means that we don't trust Him, and we will fall to fear instead of standing firm, no matter how solid the foundation beneath our feet is.

It's fairly easy for most of us to look at a fearful situation and know that God is capable of taking care of it. Most Christians don't have too much trouble believing that God can do anything He wants to do. For us, the real difficulty comes in believing that He will.

We struggle to believe that God will act in our lives on our behalf even when He clearly promises us that He will. This is the root of the problem with our trust in God. But we can overcome this struggle.

We can learn to believe God's promises to us by following the example of one very courageous Israelite leader who stood out from an unbelieving generation because of his belief in God's promises.

Long before Shadrach, Meshach, and Abednego were carried off to Babylon as slaves in the Old Testament, another generation of Israelites walked out of Egypt as a free nation for the first time in four hundred years. A mighty man of God who spoke to their heavenly Father face-to-face led those men and women.

With their own eyes, they saw God perform amazing miracles. They witnessed the waters of Egypt turned to blood and plagues of frogs and locusts appear nearly instantaneously. They observed the angel of death take the lives of the firstborn son in every Egyptian household overnight. They even saw the Red Sea stand firm by the power of God and then come crashing down on their former captors. If anyone should have been capable of trusting God and believing His promises to them, it seems it would have been these people.

Yet they didn't trust Him. God promised the Israelites a land of abundance. He assured them freedom and security if only they would step out in faith and claim their inheritance. But when belief was needed to stand firm and fight against their enemies, they refused to trust God with their lives. The Israelites failed to trust in the Lord with all their heart.

They didn't believe God's promises to them (Deuteronomy 1:32), and they spent the rest of their lives wandering in the wilderness, no longer slaves to Egypt but never truly free. They were slaves to fear.

As Christians bound up by fear and worry, we can see the same disturbing pattern in our own lives if we look close enough. We wander through the wilderness of this fearful world saved from death for eternal life, but not truly living in the abundance of peace and hope that God promises us in our temporal lives.

Out of the unbelieving generation of Israelites, two young men stood out because they believed God and His promises to their people when everyone else was too afraid to trust Him. One of those men was Joshua. After forty years surrounded by unbelievers in the wilderness, Joshua led a new generation into victory and freedom in the Promised Land because He believed God's promises to him and to his people. Joshua trusted God with all his heart, and he lived fearlessly because of it.

Joshua walked beside Moses during the forty years of wilderness wandering. He learned at the feet of one of the most well-known and respected figures in Bible history. But scripture shows Moses had one major weakness. Moses struggled to trust God in his own life.

Scripture tells us that Moses was not allowed to enter the Promised Land because of unbelief and distrust in his own heart (Numbers 20:12), so perhaps the most important lesson Joshua learned from Moses was the danger of an unbelieving heart and the blessing of developing a trusting heart.

Scripture gives insight into the motto by which Joshua seemed to live. Near the end of his life, he gathered the Israelites together and led them in a renewal of their commitment to God. He encouraged them to choose that day whom they would serve in their lives, and then he shared his own choice, "As for me and my family, we will serve the Lord" (Joshua 24:15).

Joshua chose to serve God rather than be a prisoner to Satan's snares. He chose to live by faith instead of fear, to believe God's promises to him and his people rather than doubt them. He chose to be faithful and fearless, not afraid or discouraged.

Joshua chose to do just as God had instructed him to do when He commissioned him to lead the Israelites and said to him, "Do not be afraid or discouraged, for the Lord your God is with you wherever you go" (Joshua 1:9 HCSB). Joshua chose each and every day, in every fearful circumstance he faced, to trust God to do exactly what He had promised to do.

I live with a man who does the same thing, at least most of the time. Fear and worry rarely furrow my husband's brow, unlike my own. When circumstances arise in our lives that easily send me into a panic, Toby always assures me with his simple but strong faith in God and a sentiment that I've come to expect from him in the face of my fears, "The good Lord will take care of it."

Toby doesn't just say those faith-filled words for my benefit. He believes them with all his heart. He trusts God's ability and willingness to take care of us. I used to think that my husband was simply blessed with a trusting heart, like it was gift that I just wasn't lucky enough to be given. But I've realized that isn't true. Toby's trusting heart is the result of a choice, the result of countless choices that he has made in his life.

One day, we were sitting at our kitchen table discussing a worrisome issue in our lives when he looked at me and said for at least the tenth time, "Don't worry. The good Lord will take care of it."

In my own frustration and worry, I shot back, "But how do you know that?"

His answer humbled me. Toby replied, "I don't know it, but I want to believe it. I don't see how it's going to work out, but I choose to trust God to work it out. He hasn't failed us yet."

I want to believe. I choose to trust. Suddenly I realized that the biggest difference between my husband and myself wasn't that he was somehow blessed enough to be given a trusting heart. He chose to have a trusting heart. Toby chooses to trust God, and it is evidenced in the way he lives his life, devoid of fear and worry. He's courageous and even fearless, like Joshua.

We can do the same. We can choose today—and every day after today—to believe God's promises to us. We can choose to trust Him. We can choose to be faithful and fearless just like Joshua, or we can continue to wander in a wilderness of fear.

The truth is that we've been choosing all our lives, whether we realized it or not. It's simply time for us to change our answer to the question God has asked us in midst of every single fearful circumstance we have ever faced in this life.

The Question of Faith

In Matthew 9, two blind men came to Jesus for healing, and He asked them, "Do you believe I can make you see? They told him Yes, Lord, we do. And He healed them" (Matthew 9:28–29).

Before He raised her brother Lazarus from the dead, Jesus asked Martha, "Do you believe in me? She answered Yes, Lord" (John 11:26–27). And He showed her that her belief was justified.

Ever since God revealed himself to Abraham, a man whom scripture calls the father of all who believe (Romans 4:11), He has asked humanity one simple inquiry, the question of faith. God simply asks, "Do you trust Me?"

Do you believe? Our answer to this question determines, first and foremost, whether we will join our Father in heaven for all eternity, and, second, whether we will live this temporal life He has given us in victory or defeat, thriving on the foundation of His promises to us or wandering through the wilderness of this world afraid.

In moments of fear, when Satan overwhelms us with what-ifs that grow louder by the second, if we'll listen closely enough, we'll hear the still, small voice of God whispering in our hearts, "Do you believe? Do you believe that I am capable of taking care of you through this situation and that I am willing to do just that? Do you trust Me to hold your hand and walk with you through the fire of your fears? Do you believe in Me?"

The what-ifs clamoring for our attention often drown out God's voice, but in moments of fear, we answer His question, whether we realize it or not. We choose fear, or we choose faith. We choose to trust God, or we choose not to trust Him. We choose to believe in the absolute truth of His promises to us, or we choose to worry about things we do not completely understand and cannot change on our own.

Looking back on my life, I can clearly see that, most often, though I have known the promises of scripture in my mind, I have chosen unbelief in my heart. Though I have heard God speak personal promises in my life, I have chosen to worry. Though I have been given a firm foundation of faith beneath my feet, I have allowed myself to fall to my knees in fear. In the fearful circumstances of my life, when God has whispered, "Do you believe?", my answer, most often, has been "no."

In every fearful circumstance of our lives, we answer God's question of belief, whether we consciously think about it or not. So in order for us to begin to trust God in our lives, we must determine to consciously think about it. We must determine to consciously choose to believe. We must determine to listen for His still, small voice, and when we hear God ask us, "Do you believe?", we must choose to answer, "Yes, Lord."

I know it seems difficult—maybe even impossible—but if we'll just start with a heartfelt desire to believe God and to trust Him, we'll find that everything else will fall into place.

The Poured-Out Heart

A heartfelt desire to believe becomes belief in the hands of God. We see this truth displayed in scripture when Jesus asked another person about his belief, or lack thereof.

The father of a demon-possessed child sought help for his son from Jesus's disciples, but they were unable to cast the demon out. They took the child to Jesus. The father begged, "*If* you can do anything, have compassion on us and help us" (Mark 9:22 emphasis mine).

The father's unbelief was evident in his words, and Jesus immediately confronted him with it, saying, "*If* You can? Everything is possible to the one who believes" (Mark 9:23, emphasis mine).

Confronted with his own unbelief and Jesus's bold promise that everything is possible to the one who believes, an immense desire to believe stirred within that father's heart, and scripture says he immediately cried out, "I do believe! Help my unbelief" (Mark 9:24).

In a split second, the father went from an unbelieving question to a bold declaration of belief because he wanted so desperately to believe in Jesus's ability and willingness to act in his son's life. In the time it took him to draw the breath to form the words, the father chose to believe that everything is possible to the one who believes. He desperately wanted to believe. He chose to believe. And he believed.

The unbelieving father's heartfelt desire to believe did more than spark a flame of belief in his heart. It opened his eyes to the unbelief residing there in the darkest depths of his heart. In response, he opened his heart up to God, and in a moment of humility and complete honesty, he cried out, "Help my unbelief" (Mark 9:24).

When we truly desire to believe God's promises in our own lives and begin to consciously make the choice to believe, not only does it begin to spark belief in our hearts, it opens our eyes to the unbelief that is residing there as well. If we're anything like the unbelieving father, that sudden clarity will cause us to cry out to God, "Help my unbelief."

And that is exactly the response I believe our heavenly Father is looking for. He longs to help us, but He waits for us to open our hearts to Him and cry out, "Lord, help my unbelief."

He longs for us to give him our heart—the good and the bad—and ask Him to help us trust Him with it (Proverbs 23:26). More than anything else we could ever offer God, He desires our heart so He can mend it.

Scripture tells us, "The heart is deceitful above all things and beyond cure. Who can understand it?" (Jeremiah 17:9). It doesn't sound like much of a prize. The seat of our sinfulness lies within our human heart, but that is precisely the reason God desires it so much.

Only God can cure our hearts and create in us a clean heart (Psalm 51:10) from the inherently wicked one we mistakenly desire to protect from Him. Only God can understand the human heart and mend the brokenness that exists in each one of us.

God can take our fearful, unbelieving, distrustful heart and exchange it for a trusting heart filled with a fearless faith. He can give us a courageous heart. But He will not transform our heart unless—and until—we offer it to Him willingly. Our heart is the one true sacrifice God desires from us, and it is essential to developing trust.

Of course, it's not like we can just put a bow on our heart and hand it over to God. A heart gifted to God doesn't come in one pretty little package. It is given in a million tiny pieces poured out to Him in moments of honesty and humility, in periods of fear when we desire more than anything else to trust Him completely, but we realize that we don't.

The human heart represents a depth of spirit and soul that we can barely begin to fathom in our humanity, but to fathom it is exactly what we must do in our struggle against fear so we can pour the broken pieces out, one by one, to our heavenly Father, for a healing that only He can give.

God knows our heart, whether we pour it out to Him or not. He knows every thought, every fear, every desire, and every hurt housed in every heart of every man, woman, and child from the beginning of time (2 Chronicles 6:30). God sees every dark spot of unbelief that resides within our hearts. He doesn't need us to tell Him anything about our heart for His benefit. The benefit is solely ours.

We are the ones who will walk away from the experience with the true prize, a changed heart. As we pour out our own unbelief, God will pour in belief. He will pour in trust and mend our shield of faith.

The psalmist wrote, "Trust in him at all times, O people; pour out your heart before him" (Psalm 62:8 ESV). The most meaningful step we can make toward trusting God with all our heart is to pour out our heart before Him and tell Him when we find ourselves desiring to trust Him but struggling to do so.

As we honestly pour our hearts out to God, we will begin to understand why Jeremiah called it deceitful above all things, and we will fall totally, completely, head-over-heels in love with a Savior who loves us in spite of it, a Savior who deserves our trust completely yet comforts us every time we dump our lack of trust at His nail-scarred feet.

Our heavenly Father does not expect perfection from His imperfect creation, at least not on this side of eternity. Here and now, in this imperfect life He has called us to live, He simply desires that we acknowledge our own imperfections and struggles and bring them to Him for help and healing.

The lack of trust in our heart is no different. Our heavenly Father desires for us to run to Him in the darkness of this world and pour out the distrust and unbelief that exists in each of us so He can pick up the pieces of our broken heart and mend it for us as only He can.

We noted earlier that the apostle Peter promised that God would personally restore us (1 Peter 5:10). We learned that the word *restore* in this scripture means to mend what is broken. For those of us with fearful hearts, the apostle Peter promised that God would mend our broken hearts.[6]

And that is exactly what we need in our fearful lives, a heart healed with trust by the very hand of God. We will never move from the wilderness of fearfulness and distrust in our lives if we do not confess our struggle to God, but if we do, we'll find that God will do exactly what He promised to do. He will restore us. He will mend our heart and our shield.

Dancing in the Rain

One of the most beautiful sayings I've ever heard is, "Life isn't about surviving the storm. It's about learning to dance in the rain."

I don't know about you, but I don't want to merely survive the storms of my life. I want to dance the same way I danced the hokey pokey as a child, with fearless abandon. And no ordinary partner will do either. I want to dance with the One who holds my heart in the palm of His hand and loves me in spite of its brokenness.

My realization that a lack of trust in God was at the very heart of my every fear became a turning point in my own fight against fear. It gave me a goal to travel toward. A complete trust in God became my heart's desire. I'm not there yet, but I've seen some progress. I've learned that I can dance when I put my whole self in, especially my heart.

When fear rises up in my heart, I try to remind myself to replace it with faith, to choose trust, and to choose belief in God's ability and willingness to act in my life over the unbelief that has kept me bound by fear for so long, unable to dance.

In the midst of every fearful circumstance, as I set my heart to believe, my eyes, like those of the desperate father, are opened to the unbelief in my heart. In the face of every fear, worry, and anxiety, my prayer has become the same as his, "Lord, help my unbelief!" And every time I confess my lack of trust to my heavenly Father, something miraculous warms my broken heart, trust.

Every time I pour the lack of trust in my heart out to God in prayer, He joins me in this dance, and I am amazed that the God of heaven and earth would not only take the time to listen to me pour out my lack of trust to Him, but then would comfort me in spite of it.

In these moments of heartfelt confession, I have been able to see His trustworthiness for myself. He is there for me every time I cry out to Him, take my heart to Him for healing, and take my fears to him for courage. He helps my unbelief. He mends my heart.

In the midst of your fears, when a foundation of faith rests beneath your feet but a mountain of fear still resides in your heart, run to your heavenly Father for help. Turn to God for a healing of the heart that only He can provide.

That is the answer. When we give our heavenly Father every piece of our broken heart, God will help us to trust Him with all our heart (Proverbs 3:5). And we will learn to dance, even in the midst of the rain and the fearful storms of this life.

Chapter 9

Finding Peace of Mind

For many years I have been blessed to know an amazing minister of the gospel. This man, an evangelist at heart, has reached countless souls for Christ by asking one simple question of every single person he comes into contact with on a daily basis, "Do you know that Jesus loves you?"

Because he has witnessed it more times than he can count in his eighty-plus years, Bro. Dale Rickman knows that an understanding of God's great love for a person can change that person's life in an instant, and his most powerful message is simple. "Jesus loves you … and you … and you … "

Jesus does love you. And He loves me. Jesus loves each one of us with an eternal love that we, in our humanity, cannot fully comprehend, but even our limited understanding of God's awe-inspiring love for us is life changing.

Our understanding of God's love for us personally enables us to cast fear completely out of our lives and receive from our heavenly Father an indescribable peace that surpasses our understanding and then guards our hearts and minds to boot (Philippians 4:7). And that is exactly what we need to mend our shield of faith, a peace that will guard our hearts and minds against our enemy's flaming arrows of fear.

Jesus promised He would leave this peace here on earth as a gift for us (John 14:27). Though it may seem elusive to those of us who struggle with fear, peace can be found right where Jesus left it, where our limited understanding meets God's limitless understanding, through the practice of prayer.

God's Greatest Gift

God loves us so much that He gave His one and only Son as a sacrifice, an atonement that provides forgiveness for our sins, so that whoever believes in Him will be saved (John 3:16). God's love for us provides our salvation and our peace.

There are two kinds of peace in the Christian walk of faith, peace with God and peace in God. Peace with God is the peace we receive at the moment of our salvation. To have peace with God simply means that we have been cleansed by the blood of Christ and sealed for the day of redemption. Through this priceless peace, we gain access to our heavenly Father.

Peace in God is the peace that floods our hearts and minds as we learn to walk through this fearful life by our faith instead of our fear. We receive the precious gift of peace in God when we lean completely on our heavenly Father's power and wisdom in the fearful and worrisome circumstances of our lives.

Before we can ever have peace in God, we must have peace with God. Peace with God enables us to receive God's peace in everything else. Peace with God is simple to obtain because it is tied to our salvation, which is a free gift from God, available to anyone, anywhere, anytime. For some of us, however, it's not quite so simple to experience.

Perhaps the most common obstacle to experiencing peace in our daily lives is that even those of us who have peace with God often, in the darkest corners of our minds, doubt that we do. We question whether we really belong to God. We wonder if, when it comes down to it, God will really forgive the darkness that we know exists in us.

When the writer of Hebrews wrote about those who were held in slavery all their lives by the fear of death (Hebrews 2:15), it's possible that he was speaking about children of God who had yet to wrap their minds around their own salvation and unwrap the peace of God in their lives.

The Greek word used for death in Hebrews 2:15, *thanatos*, has an implied reference to a future in hell. The final definition is in the widest sense, death comprising all the miseries arising from sin as well as physical death … to be followed by wretchedness in hell.[7] It stands to reason that the overwhelming fear of death stems, at least in part, from the fear of spending eternity lost in the wretchedness of hell.

Our greatest fear, because death is our greatest fear for many of us, may be rooted in insecurity regarding what should be our greatest source of peace, our eternal salvation.

We claim Christianity. We hope we're saved. But deep in our minds, we doubt that we really are. We wonder if we'll awaken to an eternity in hell after our physical death. We wonder if we really are saved, if we really are forgiven and loved.

No matter how many times we hear that Jesus loves us and that we were forgiven at Calvary's hill, some of us just can't seem to get it through our thick skulls, and we fail to experience the peace of our salvation.

When we lack a sense of peace in regards to our salvation, it is highly unlikely that we'll experience God's peace in other aspects of our lives. Our peace with God ensures that we can have peace in the midst of every fearful situation in our lives instead of fear, anxiety, and worry.

The Jimmy Needham song, "Forgiven and Loved," speaks to our struggle to experience peace. The lyrics tell of a peace that has almost passed away. The singer seems to beg for an assurance of salvation by pleading for his heavenly Father to tell me I'm forgiven and loved. This song speaks to me because I know exactly what it's like to doubt my own salvation. Perhaps you do too.

For years, I worried that I would never be good enough to be saved, and every time I fell into a pit of sin, I feared that I might have blown my last chance at salvation. But when I fell on my knees in a moment of desperation and pleaded with God, like the singer above, to tell me I'm forgiven and loved, my heavenly Father did just that.

God didn't explain my salvation to me in words. He didn't lecture me over the ins and outs of receiving eternal life. He simply closed the gap between my understanding and His, and I knew, beyond a shadow of a doubt, I was saved. I knew I belonged to Him. I knew I was forgiven and loved. My heavenly Father gave me a peace in that moment that I cannot describe and assured me of my own salvation.

I'd like to say that was the end of that, but it wasn't. My doubts resurfaced, and my peace nearly passed away, but when I asked God again to tell me I was forgiven and loved, His peace flooded my mind a second time … and again the next time. It's been a long time since I've had to ask God for an assurance of my own salvation, but if the need arises, I know He will give me that same understanding and that same peace again.

God does not intend for us to doubt our salvation for one moment after we receive it. But if we do, in the weakness of our humanity, doubt the gift of salvation that He so graciously gives, in His infinite mercy, He will not withhold from us an assurance of our own salvation.

Our heavenly Father will tell each of us that we are forgiven and loved and that we are saved. And He will give us the understanding that we need to move forward in our lives with peace.

Scripture tells us, "This is how we know that we remain in Him and He in us: He has given assurance to us from His Spirit" (I John 4:13 HCSB). In his infinite patience, God will help us to know beyond a shadow of a doubt that we remain in Him and He in us by giving us assurance from His Spirit as many times as it takes for us to have peace in our salvation. And we desperately need that peace as an active part of our faith.

If you believe that you are a Christian but don't have peace in your own salvation, pray for it. Do not move from where you are sitting until you are assured of your own salvation by the Spirit of God that resides in you. And the next time you doubt, ask God to tell you again and again, if that's what it takes.

If you are not a Christian but you desire to become one, again, pray. Confess your belief in Christ Jesus, His death, and resurrection (Romans 10:9). Find a church family and get involved because that is His desire for all of us.

Do not spend another moment of your life devoid of the peace that God promises is wrapped within the gift of your salvation. Our heavenly Father will give us an understanding of our own salvation when we ask Him to, as many times as we need Him to until we have the peace He promises us.

In his second letter to Timothy, the apostle Paul wrote, "God has not given us a spirit of fear, but of power and of love and of a sound mind" (2 Timothy 1:7). Through His Spirit, God will give us a sound mind of peace in our own salvation to begin to mend our shield of faith (Psalm 18:35). But that peace is only the beginning.

The Prayer of Peace

Whether we are searching for peace in our salvation or peace in our lives, prayer is the pathway toward the peace of God, which surpasses all understanding and then guards our hearts and minds as an added bonus.

Scripture tells us, "Do not be anxious about anything, but in everything by prayer and supplication with thanksgiving, let your requests be made known to God. And the peace of God, which surpasses all understanding, will guard your hearts and minds in Christ Jesus" (Philippians 4:6–7).

In every circumstance that causes us fear, worry, or anxiety, the Word of God tells us to let our requests be made known to our heavenly Father in prayer. When we pour our requests out to our heavenly Father in prayer, scripture tells us that His peace will come to our hearts and minds.

If you're like me, you've done this. You've prayed time and time again in countless worrisome circumstances and fearful situations, and you've found that, despite your best efforts, peace hasn't always followed your prayers. Perhaps the elusiveness of peace has to do with the focus of our requests. What we pray for in moments of fear determines how much peace we experience in those moments.

I don't know about you, but most often, when I'm worried or scared, what I desire more than anything else is for God to take away the object of my fear, and my prayers tend to focus on that. The problem is that God doesn't promise to remove the fearful situations in our lives. He promises to give us peace in the midst of them.

The apostle Paul wrote about a thorn in his flesh, which we can compare to our fears. Paul prayed three times for God to remove the thorn completely from his life, but God refused. He told Paul that His strength shone in Paul's weakness.

The fearful and worrisome circumstances in our lives that we desire more than anything for God to remove may be the stage upon which His strength will shine the most brilliantly in our lives. If all our prayers revolve around removing that situation, we may never experience God's power and His peace in the midst of it.

The psalmist wrote, "Your eyes saw me when I was formless; all (my) days were written in Your book and planned before a single one of them began" (Psalm 139:16 HCSB). God has a unique plan for each of us, a magnificent plan that includes every day, every hour, and every moment of our lives.

There's nothing wrong with praying that God would remove fearful and worrisome circumstances from our lives or the lives of others, but in order to experience His peace, we must be open to the possibility that He won't. The realization of our worst fears may be a part of His plan for our lives.

I have no doubt that, if the silent prayers of Shadrach, Meshach, and Abednego were recorded in the moments before King Nebuchadnezzar threw them into the fiery furnace, they would have included a request to avoid that furnace. But afterward, after Jesus showed up in the midst of the flames and walked them out the other side, fearless and fireproof, I doubt they would have traded that experience for anything in the world.

Some of the most beautiful treasures in this life are experienced in the most difficult moments, and if those times are removed from our lives, the treasures must be removed as well. If God removed all the fires from our lives at our request, we would never see the beauty He desires to bring forth from the ashes (Isaiah 61:3). Sometimes we must experience the realization of our fears.

After avoidance, perhaps our second most common request in moments of fear is for understanding. When anxiety rules in our lives and peace is nowhere to be found, we start to think that, if we could just wrap our minds more completely around the worrisome situation we're dealing with, we would gain some peace over it. So we pray for understanding.

Unfortunately, when we depend on our own understanding for peace, we experience very little peace in our lives. There are countless fearful situations in this life that we do not completely understand. Fortunately God promises us a peace that surpasses our own understanding, especially for the situations in our lives that are difficult or impossible to understand.

The well-known proverb that tells us to trust in the Lord with all our heart continues by specifically instructing us *not* to rely on our own understanding (Proverbs 3:5, emphasis mine). The unspoken instruction is to rely on God's understanding, which, unlike our own, is limitless (Isaiah 40:28).

Our heavenly Father tells us in scripture, "My thoughts are not your thoughts, and your ways are not My ways. For as heaven is higher than earth, so My ways are higher than your ways, and My thoughts than your thoughts" (Isaiah 55:8–9).

God understands the most frightening situations in our lives. He knows when they can actually bring something good into our lives (Romans 8:28). He sees how the impossible can become possible through His power at work in our lives (Mark 9:23). God understands all the things we don't, and we can lean on His understanding when our own runs out.

In moments of fear and worry, we make countless requests of God, and we should. I don't think our heavenly Father ever grows weary of hearing our requests, but one simple request, which perhaps we're not making, has the potential to flood our hearts and minds with the peace of God. When we request to know and to understand our heavenly Father's love for us, we unwrap the gift of His peace.

Perfect Love

Our heavenly Father loves each one of us with an eternal love that we, in our humanity, cannot fully comprehend, but we must attempt to grasp it because our understanding, limited though it may be, of God's awe-inspiring love for us gives us the ability to cast fear completely out of our lives and receive peace for our minds.

As Christians, we know that God's love for us provides our peace with God and our eternal salvation through the sacrifice made on Calvary's hill, but what we may not fully grasp is that God's love for us provides our temporal salvation and our peace in God—our peace in this life—as well.

In a well-known verse of scripture, the beloved apostle John wrote, "There is no fear in love, but perfect love casts out fear" (1 John 4:18). It's easy to see what this verse means on the surface. When we love someone with an unconditional, perfect love, we will face any fear to save that person. Nearly every parent I know would be able to instantly cast out his or her fear of death to step in front a bullet that was intended for his or her child.

But there's a deeper truth hidden in this scripture that has nothing to do with our own capacity to love and everything to do with God's perfect love for us, His children. The two verses of scripture prior to the one that speaks of casting out fear says, "We have come to know and to believe the love that God has for us" (1 John 4:16) and "by this is love perfected with us" (1 John

4:17). In other words, love becomes perfected in us as we come to know and believe the love that God has for us.

When we know and believe that God loves us on a deeply personal level, His love is perfected in us, and we come to understand that our heavenly Father's perfect love for us will cause Him to step in front of every bullet that's aimed at us and save us, just as any loving parent would save his or her child.

Scripture tells us that the righteous person faces many troubles, but the Lord comes to the rescue each time (Psalm 34:19 NLT). Our heavenly Father rescues us in the midst of every fearful situation we face in this life because He loves us.

Sometimes God will rescue us completely from the object of our fear, and our salvation will be that we avoid the thing we fear the most. Other times our salvation will simply be that God Himself will personally hold our hand and walk with us in the midst of the fire, teaching us, guiding us, and growing us in His image, as He did for Shadrach, Meshach, and Abednego.

In whatever way our heavenly Father chooses to rescue us, we can be certain that He will always save us in every fearful circumstance we face because of His perfect love for us. When we know beyond a shadow of a doubt that God will save us because He loves us, we gain the ability to cast fear completely out of our lives, as the beloved apostle John described in the scriptures above.

The Greek word translated as *casts* in the phrase, "perfect love casts out fear," means to throw or let go of a thing without caring where it falls or to give over to one's care, uncertain about the result.[8]

Perfect love casts out fear when we willingly give our fears over to our heavenly Father's care and throw our anxieties at His feet because, though we remain uncertain about what our future holds, we are certain that His love for us will cause Him to save us.

Perfect Peace

When we cast our fears at God's feet, not only will He save us, He will give us, in return for our worry and anxiety, the added bonus of peace that surpasses understanding and guards our hearts and minds.

The apostle Peter tells us that we can cast all our anxieties on God because He cares so deeply for us, and then a few verses later in a scripture that we keep coming back to, he tells us that, as we seek to stand firm in the strength of our faith, God will support us. We learned earlier that the word *support* means that God will stabilize our minds (1 Peter 5:7, 10).

Our heavenly Father will stabilize our minds with His peace when we cast our anxieties at His feet because we know beyond a shadow of a doubt that His great love for us will cause Him to save us. Peace comes to us when we know that God loves us and His love for us will be our salvation. But as we already noted in our struggle to accept our own salvation, we often experience difficulty in knowing and understanding our heavenly Father's love for us.

We are right back where we started, wrapped up in the midst of our own struggle to believe that Jesus loves us personally, even on our worst day. The answer to our dilemma remains the same. We must ask Him to tell us that we are forgiven and loved.

When fearful circumstances arise in our lives, the one request that has greatest potential to bring peace to our minds is when we ask God to tell us that He loves us—when we ask God to help us know and believe the love that He has for us—so we can cast our fears at His feet with the certainty that He will save us.

The apostle Paul prayed a prayer for the members of the church at Ephesus. He wrote that he knelt before the Father and prayed for them that they might be strengthened with power in the inner man through God's Spirit and that they might be able to comprehend the length, width, height, and depth of God's love and to know the love of Christ that surpasses knowledge so they would be filled with all the fullness of God (Ephesians 3:17–19 NLT).

I can almost picture Paul on his knees before God, praying for the members of the church to understand God's love for them. I'm sure there were times when he prayed that prayer for himself as well. Like Bro. Dale Rickman and the apostle John, the apostle Paul knew that a personal understanding of God's love has the power to change lives.

God's love for us is beyond our comprehension, but when we request in prayer a more complete understanding of His love for us, our heavenly Father will meet our limited understanding with His limitless understanding and help us to know the love of Christ that surpasses knowledge so we can exchange our fears for the fullness of His peace and the strength of a more complete faith in Him.

Paul's prayer is taped to my bathroom mirror so I will see it daily. I pray this prayer for myself and for those near and dear to me as often as I think about it because, when life gets worrisome and circumstances get fearful, we need to know one thing above all else, Jesus loves us.

That knowledge helps us to understand that God will save us and gives us the ability to cast fear completely out of our lives and experience God's perfect peace in our minds. Scripture says that God will keep the one whose mind is focused on Him in perfect peace (Isaiah 26:3).

When the focus of our prayers becomes less about ourselves and our fears and more about knowing our heavenly Father and His love for us through every circumstance we face in this life, His perfect peace will fill our minds, and our shield of faith will have one less hole.

Chapter 10

Anchoring Hope for the Soul

I have an issue with my heart that causes it to beat a little too fast at times. It's a fairly common problem, and most of the time, it's well controlled with medication, so I didn't think much about it when my husband and I decided we should purchase extra life insurance for both of us several years ago.

We did a little research, found a company we liked, and then filled out the necessary forms. A few days later, a very friendly nurse visited our home for a brief physical. A couple of weeks after that, we received a letter in the mail, informing us that, even though my husband had been approved, I had been rejected.

Without a moment's pause, we started the process again with a different company. I honestly figured that the rejection was a mistake. But when the second company rejected me, I realized there was no error.

Still, we tried again and then again. That fourth rejection left me feeling rather hopeless. I spent a little too much time wondering whether those faceless people who analyze risk for insurance companies might be correct in their obvious assessment that I don't have the greatest chance of living to old age.

I laughingly told myself and those around me that they had failed to consider my eternal guarantee, but it didn't help because the truth is that, when I think about my life and my death, more often than not, I fail to consider my own eternal guarantee. And I have a feeling that I'm not alone.

Though we, as Christians, are destined for an eternal paradise, we tend to place all our hope in this life rather than the next. We hope that God will save us from every fearful circumstance we face. We hope that He will walk beside us daily and make His presence known to us in every difficulty. We hope that God will enable us to live a very long and fruitful life to His glory.

We hope in our future on this Earth, but we don't hope in eternity. We limit our hope to the life we see around us, but our hope is not meant to be limited to things we can see (Romans 8:24). The apostle Paul wrote, "If our hope is limited to this life, we are of all people most to be pitied" (1 Corinthians 15:19). Let that sink in for a moment.

We are a pitiful people if we limit our hope to this life. Our hope was never meant to be limited to this life. Our hope is eternal, and it is meant to give strength to the piece of eternity that God Himself has placed within each of us, our eternal soul (Ecclesiastes 3:11).

Our hope is meant to stretch past this life and into eternity toward things that we cannot completely understand and can only barely begin to imagine. Our hope is meant to be more than our eyes can see, more than our ears can hear, and more than has ever entered the human mind (1 Corinthians 2:9). Our hope is meant to give substance to our faith (Hebrews 11:1), but when we limit our eternal hope to our temporal lives, we cripple our faith.

When we fail to consider our eternal guarantee, our hope fails us, and the shield of faith that is meant to be invincible becomes vulnerable to our enemy's flaming arrows of fear. To mend our shield of faith, we must make eternity a part of our temporal lives so hope will come alive in us.

Eternal Hope

Ecclesiastes 3:11 says God has made everything appropriate in its time. He has also put eternity in their hearts, but man cannot discover the work God has done from beginning to end.

We are eternal beings, and that knowledge has a resting place in our hearts. The very hand of God put it there. We may not consciously think about it much, but every human being knows deep within our souls that we are meant for more than this world. Our souls are eternal, and our hearts and minds know it on some level.

Imagine for a moment how tormenting that subconscious knowledge of eternity could be in the life of an unbeliever. It would indeed be a nameless fear, a terror that could not be explained or understood, but existed deep within the soul.

As Christians, on the other hand, we can be assured that we will live forever with God in heaven, but as the scripture above states, we cannot discover the work God has done from beginning to end. We don't understand what lies in eternity. We can't comprehend it. And though scripture paints some beautiful pictures, they are few in number and lacking in detail.

Eternity stretches out like a nearly blank canvas in the hands of a magnificent artist. We know that what He paints will be breathtaking, but we cannot picture it in our own minds. Only the artist can see the painting before it is completed.

Looking toward that canvas can be incredibly frightening to our human hearts and minds. The sheer infinite possibilities overwhelm us and can even make us fearful of an eternal salvation that should be our greatest source of hope.

For many of us, fear circles the end of our temporal lives like a dark cloud that we can't see past. We fear the end of this life. We fear death. Some of us worry endlessly that hell might be our final destination. (Hopefully we conquered that worry in chapter nine.) For others, the mere thought of eternity fills us with dread instead of hope.

I remember sitting on a church pew as a young child, listening to the preacher talk about the glorious rewards of heaven and the terrible punishment of hell. Both options sounded rather frightening to me because the concept of eternity scared me to death. The thought of spending forever (and ever and ever and ever) anywhere gave me a terrible knot deep in the pit of my stomach and made me want to throw up.

Even after I put my hope in Christ for my salvation, the hope I knew I was supposed to have in heaven always seemed a little more like fear to me. I imagine Satan danced a little jig on cloud nine as his snare of fear stole every ounce of hope from the eternal salvation that Jesus died to give me. I'm sure he's danced a few such jigs because somehow I don't think I'm alone. In fact, I know I'm not.

My father-in-law, Jirden, was just like me and perhaps even worse. He had an overwhelming fear of death, but in the last few months of his life, he overcame that fear in spectacular fashion.

On Christmas Eve several years ago, while still reeling from the sudden loss of a loved one, my family and I learned that Jirden had kidney cancer. A few weeks later, he underwent surgery to remove a football-sized tumor that was wrapped around his entire right kidney. During the extremely long and involved surgery, Jirden crashed. His body gave up on life, but the doctors were able to revive him in time.

When Jirden woke up in the ICU a few days later, he told an amazing story. He had seen the pearly gates of heaven, where a host of friends and family members had gathered to greet him upon his arrival. He had felt the peace that surpasses all understanding when he saw their smiling faces and heard their laughter echoing around him.

Jirden couldn't wait to tell everyone he knew about his glimpse of heaven, but the most powerful aspect of his experience wasn't the story he told. It was the change in him. Jirden had been terrified of death for his entire life. He hated to visit hospitals, nursing homes, or doctor's offices. He refused to attend funerals unless it was absolutely necessary, and then he bolted for the door the moment he could escape. His fear of death was no ordinary fear. It was an overwhelming terror that was known to all who knew him well.

But Jirden brought a hope home from his brief visit to heaven, and he shared it with everyone he knew. His cancer returned almost immediately after his surgery, and he died less than four months later, but during the final months of his life on earth, he became a living, breathing example of eternal hope.

Every person he spoke to in that time was forever changed by his firsthand account of heaven and the dramatic change in his life from a fearful man to a fearless witness of the hope of heaven.

Jirden's glimpse of heaven filled him with an eternal hope. His hope was no longer limited to the temporal life around him. It stretched into the eternal and gave him a strength of soul and a fearless faith that was absolutely awe-inspiring, especially to those who knew him best.

Though we can't orchestrate a near-death experience—and, really, who would want to do that anyway—we can glimpse heaven and bring hope home with us. We can experience an eternal hope in our own lives by peering past the point where our temporal hope stops, the end of this life.

Glimpsing Heaven

In my own life, like Jirden's, the fear of death has been an overwhelming fear all my life. Even as I began to stand firm against other fears, the fear of death remained the one tormenting fear that would not be completely overcome.

The enemy of my soul would walk me to the edge of a cliff in my mind, time and time again. He would threaten to push me over it, though the power was not his to wield. He would threaten death, and I would cower in terror every time until one day I took all the power out of his threat and jumped over the edge of the cliff in my own mind. I contemplated what my death would really mean.

Immediately my thoughts turned to those I would leave behind, and the source of my own fears overwhelmed me. Just then, I heard God whisper, as though He was speaking within the very depths of my soul, "I would take care of them."

I thought of how God has guided me throughout my life. I knew I would never be ready to leave my loved ones behind. I realized that, if God called me home that day, I could trust Him to take care of them in ways I never could. And that gave me hope.

Next, my thoughts turned to my own fate. As a I child of God, I knew I would immediately be in heaven after my death, but honestly, the thought filled me with fear, not hope, and I knew that was where my deepest, darkest fear resided, where my hope should live instead.

I feared eternity, heaven, and all the things I could not see, feel, touch, or even begin to imagine. So, inspired by my father-in-law's life and death, I sought to glimpse what I could not envision.

It only took a brief glimpse of heaven to fill Jirden with hope instead of fear, and I thought, *Perhaps the same could be true for me.* I read through the apostle John's scriptural account of heaven in Revelation 4–5 and tried to imagine what it would be like to see heaven with my own eyes.

I imagined what it would be like to see a new heaven and a new earth, the Holy City, and the New Jerusalem and to hear a loud voice from the throne of God saying, "Look! God's dwelling place is now among the people, and He will dwell with them. They will be his people, and God himself will be with them and be their God. He will wipe every tear from their eyes. There will be no more death or mourning or crying or pain" (Revelation 21:1–4 NIV).

I began to pray for an eternal hope to replace my fear of eternity. Scripture tells us to set our sights on the realities of heaven, where Christ sits in the place of honor at God's right hand, and to think about the things of heaven, not the things of earth, because our real life is hidden with Christ in God (Colossians 3:1–3).

In order to experience hope the way God intends for us to experience in this life, we must do just that, even if, perhaps especially if, it scares us to death. We must set our minds, our hearts, and our souls on heaven. Imagine eternity. Picture the throne room of God in your mind's eye. Set your sights on the realities of heaven (Colossians 3:2).

In the words of the apostle Paul, I pray that your hearts will be flooded with light so you can understand the confident hope He has given to you (Ephesians 1:18 NLT) and your soul may be strengthened with your own eternal hope.

Anchoring Hope

Imagining heaven may seem a little weird, but when we set our sights on our heavenly home, we are doing exactly what the Bible's greatest heroes of faith did, so perhaps living a life of faith calls for a little weirdness.

The author of Hebrews, in a chapter of scripture that is commonly referred to as the faith chapter of the Bible, wrote that, as the great men and women of scripture accomplished God's will for their lives, they had their sights set on the realities of heaven. The great heroes of faith proclaimed that they were foreigners and strangers on earth, and they were longing for a better country, a heavenly one (Hebrews 11:13, 16). Their hope was not limited to this earth. It lay in eternity. They longed for their heavenly home. The Greek word for *longing* used in this scripture means to stretch one's self out in order to touch or to grasp something and to reach after or desire something.[9]

All of the heroes of faith in scripture had their feet firmly planted on Earth, accomplishing amazing acts for the kingdom of God, but their hearts, minds, and souls were stretched out toward heaven in hope.

Earlier in the same book of scripture, the author beautifully illustrated this concept when he called our hope a strong and trustworthy anchor for our souls that leads us through the curtain into God's inner sanctuary (Hebrews 6:19 NLT).

Hope originates in eternity—in the presence of God—but it flows backward through time. We experience eternal hope in our lives when we stretch our hearts and minds out toward heaven and anchor our souls in the depths of the magnificent crystal sea that lies at the foot of throne of God (Revelation 4:6).

This eternal hope gives strength to our soul and becomes an essential part of our shield of faith. It enables us to stand firm amid all the fears of life that threaten to sweep us off our feet because it helps us to realize that this world is not our home. Heaven is.

The apostle Paul wrote that, as Christians, we are citizens of heaven (Philippians 3:20). From the very moment that we become children of God, we no longer belong to this world. Heaven is our home.

In order to experience hope the way we're meant to and live by our faith instead of our fear, we must stop thinking of ourselves as temporal beings with a tiny piece of eternity residing in our hearts and begin to think of ourselves as eternal beings dwelling in a temporal tent of a body (2 Peter 1:13) for a short and sometimes fearful walk on this Earth.

We must embrace the eternal existence that the hand of God has placed within us (Ecclesiastes 3:11) and begin to look forward to eternity, our true home, with a sense of awe, wonder, and excitement, just like the Bible's great heroes of faith did. Just like Jesus did (Hebrews 12:2).

We are strangers (1 Peter 2:11) in a strange, heartbreaking, and fearful land, and when we really grasp that truth for ourselves, we will grasp our eternal hope and become anchored to heaven by it.

Temporal Hope

Our true and eternal hope lies in heaven, and it can only be found there, but since we are living a temporal life, we need a temporal hope as well.

This life can seem pretty hopeless at times. Bad things happen to the best of people, and sometimes our worst fears do come to pass. Jesus Himself warned us that in this life we would have trials and sorrows, but He followed that statement by giving us hope in the fact that He overcame this world (John 16:33).

We can too. Our greatest hope for this life is that we might, like Jesus, overcome this world and, in doing so, become a source of hope to those around us. The apostle Peter did. Like us, he struggled with fear, but like Jesus, he overcame and became a source of hope. His example offers temporal hope to us.

Before he became the fearless man of faith who authored two encouraging letters to the early church in an effort to help them overcome their own valid fears of persecution, Peter's own struggles with fear are recorded in scripture. In Luke's account of the night of the crucifixion, the apostle Peter's fall to the snare of fear is poured out in black and white for all the world to see.

That night, Jesus revealed to Peter, Satan had asked to sift him as wheat, but that He, Himself, had prayed for Peter, that his faith should not fail. Then, Jesus lovingly and gracefully instructed Peter, when you have returned to Me, strengthen your brethren (Luke 22:31–32 NIV).

Immediately the apostle Peter, not yet humbled by his own experience, replied, "Lord, I am ready to go with you to prison and to death" (Luke 22:33). But when it came down to it later that night, he wasn't.

Peter was terrified of death, and his actions displayed his fear. He cowered in front of a mere servant girl. He denied Christ not once or twice, but three times in a matter of a few hours. But Jesus knew that Peter would deny him long before he did. He told Peter, "Before the rooster crows today, you will deny three times that you know me" (Luke 22:34). A few verses later, we find Peter weeping bitterly with the sound of the rooster crowing and the words of Jesus ringing in his head (Luke 22:61–62). Peter fell to fear that night, and though that wasn't the first time, it might have been the last.

Our heavenly Father knew that Peter would struggle with fear and that his faith would falter but not fail. He also knew that Peter would be changed forever when he glimpsed the eternal in his risen Savior, Jesus Christ. God knew that Peter would become the bold (Acts 4:13) leader of the early church whose changed life would be showcased in the book of Acts and his own epistles.

God's plan for Peter's life took into account his struggle with fear and his triumph over it. He planned for Peter's life to be a light to all of us who struggle with fear and look to scripture for help and hope. That's exactly why Jesus instructed Peter to strengthen his brothers with his own eternal hope and his strengthened shield of faith after he had overcome his fears and returned to Him (Luke 22:32).

Peter did just that. The apostle Peter wrote the words that have become the foundation for this entire book.

> Give all your worries and cares to God, for he cares about you. Stay alert! Watch out for your great enemy, the devil. He prowls around like a roaring lion, looking for someone to devour. Stand firm against him, and be strong in your faith. Remember that your Christian brothers and sisters all over the world are going through the same kind of suffering you are. In his kindness God called you to share in his eternal glory by means of Christ Jesus. So after you have suffered a little while, he will restore, support, and strengthen you, and he will place you on a firm foundation (1 Peter 5:7–10 NLT).

Among other things that we've already discussed, Peter promised that, as we seek to stand firm against our fears, as he exemplified in his life, God will personally strengthen us. God will strengthen our souls with hope, and He will do it through Peter's words, if we'll let him.

Peter's writings have been a source of personal strength to me. His words have given me hope that a strong and invincible faith is possible even in the life of someone like me, who has fallen repeatedly to fear. The scriptures above have become a lifeline of temporal hope in my own battle against fear.

I hope that these scriptures have become a lifeline of hope in your life as well. As you've read the apostle Peter's words mixed with mine through the pages of this book, my greatest hope is that these words have strengthened you with the hope that you can overcome your own fears. And I hope you share that hope with those around you.

When I contemplate Peter's life and the impact his words have had on my life, I can't help but think that our greatest hope for this life is not about what we can get, but what we can give. We can give hope to those around us by overcoming fear in our own lives. Each of us can be like the apostle Peter. We can strengthen our brethren with the example of victory in our own lives. And, really, what more could we possibly hope for?

Our struggle with fear is not a hopeless battle. It is our chance to hold up an invincible shield of faith and become a hero of faith in our own time. In this temporal life we're living, our greatest hope is to overcome our fears by our faith and become a source of hope to others.

And we can. We can overcome our fears by our faith in our heavenly Father.

All praise to God, the Father of our Lord Jesus Christ.
God is our merciful Father and the source of all comfort.
He comforts us in all our troubles so that we can
comfort others. When they are troubled, we will be able
to give them the same comfort God has given us.
—2 Corinthians 1:3–4

About the Author

 Charity A. Lane is a wife to Toby, a mother to TJ and Toby Jo, and a child of the one true God. She is also a nurse who believes that the greatest purpose in this life is to help fellow humans through the most difficult struggles of life. This purpose inspired her to write Faith over Fear, and Charity believes that by chronicling her own struggle with fear and sharing the lessons she's learned about overcoming fear through faith, she will be able to help others through their own struggles with fear.

Endnotes

1 Microsoft Corporation, Encarta® World English Dictionary (North American Edition)(2009), http://encarta.msn.com/dictionary_/Fear.html.

2 James Strong, *Strong's Exhaustive Concordance of the Bible* (Nashville: Broadman & Homan Publishing, 1999), #2675.

3 James Strong, *Strong's Exhaustive Concordance of the Bible* (Nashville: Broadman & Homan Publishing, 1999), #4741.

4 James Strong, *Strong's Exhaustive Concordance of the Bible* (Nashville: Broadman & Homan Publishing, 1999), #4599.

5 James Strong. *Strong's Exhaustive Concordance of the Bible* (Nashville: Broadman & Homan Publishing, 1999), #2311, #2310.

6 James Strong, *Strong's Exhaustive Concordance of the Bible* (Nashville: Broadman & Homan Publishing, 1999), #2675.

7 James Strong, *Strong's Exhaustive Concordance of the Bible* (Nashville: Broadman & Homan Publishing, 1999), #2288.

8 James Strong, *Strong's Exhaustive Concordance of the Bible* (Nashville: Broadman & Homan Publishing, 1999), #906.

9 James Strong, *Strong's Exhaustive Concordance of the Bible* (Nashville: Broadman & Homan Publishing, 1999), #3977.

Printed in the United States
By Bookmasters